Francis Albert Prince

The Genealogy of the Prince family

From 1660 to 1899

Francis Albert Prince

The Genealogy of the Prince family
From 1660 to 1899

ISBN/EAN: 9783337170196

Printed in Europe, USA, Canada, Australia, Japan

Cover: Foto ©ninafisch / pixelio.de

More available books at **www.hansebooks.com**

THE
GENEALOGY

—OF THE—

PRINCE FAMILY.
FROM 1660 TO 1899.

COMPILED, ARRANGED AND PUBLISHED
—BY—
FRANK A. PRINCE,
DANIELSON, CONN.

J. H. BRIGGS, PRINTER,
DANIELSON, CONN.
1899.

Copyright, 1899,
BY
FRANK A. PRINCE.
All rights reserved.

1243974

CONTENTS.

	PAGE.
Descendants of Daniel Prince	5 to 12
Robert Prince, of Salem, and His Descendants	12 to 113
Thompson's First Ministers	113
Records of Other Prince Families	115 to 120
Richard Johnston Prince and His Descendants	120 to 124
Prince Records, or Information for those who shall follow after	124 to 129
Corrections	129
Additional Records	130 to 131
Remarks	132
Index, by the Name of Prince	133 to 140
Index of Names other than Prince	140 to 153

LIST OF ILLUSTRATIONS.

	FACING PAGE.
Frank A. Prince............Frontispiece.	
Daniel and James Prince	5
Robert Prince House	13
Lyman Prince	41
Nathan Prince House	50
Daniel Prince	52
Col. Edward Prince	64
Albert Prince House	73
Albert Prince	76
Ophelia (Elliott) Prince	77
William Prince	80
Robert Prince House	82
Frank A. Prince House, Home of the Author	98
Sarah Maria (Chaffee) Prince	100
Nathan Dyer Prince	104
Charles Henry Prince	112
Annie Bell (Bright) Prince	113

PREFACE.

In compiling a work of this kind, gathering genealogical data from so many different sources, no one only those who have had some experience in this line of work, has any adequate idea of the amount of time, labor, and expense that is consumed in investigation and research, which is requisite for a full and complete record. Many embarrassments are encountered which give the compiler no little anxiety, especially so in some of the correspondence and records that have been received from many friends and interested parties, which were better than the average, yet some have been so illegible that great care and due diligence have been exercised to avoid as many errors as possible in the compilation of this work, but undoubtedly some will be found. It is impossible to get every date correct, there being so many discrepancies in records of dates and names.

To many unacquainted with genealogical information, many of the items or records contained herein, though very valuable and interesting, may seem too trivial or too much beneath what is called the "dignity of history" to be inserted, yet it may be observed, that we are not entirely competent judges of what may be valuable or interesting to those who shall come after us. Instead of polished sentences, or well turned periods, *truth in its simplicity* should be the aim of the genealogist and historian. A person can *write* a book in a very short time, but there is *not a person* that will ever live long enough to gather all the records and important data which might be found concerning the Prince family since their emigration to this country to the present time.

PREFACE.

The study of genealogy is so very fascinating that the compiler has considered the task of gathering what is contained herein a pleasure rather than a burden, although it is far from being complete, and far from being what the compiler might desire. It is hoped, however, that it may stimulate some future historian or genealogist to collect the stray threads of family life and gather them into completeness, and to such the compiler would say that he has in his possession a large amount of valuable information, not herein contained, which would be of great utility to those contemplating the same. Hoping that this little volume will meet the approval of the present generation who give it a perusal, and of the generations which are to follow, and that any corrections or additions will be kindly forwarded to the compiler, is the wish of

THE AUTHOR.

Danielson, Conn., 1899.

EXPLANATION.

The few abbreviations used in this work will be easily understood:

    a.—for about.
    b.—for born.
    d.—for died.
    dau.—for daughter.
    m.—for married.
    wid.—for widow.
    g. s.—for gravestone.
    I, II, III, IV, V, &c., indicate the generations.

DANIEL AND JAMES PRINCE.
[TWINS.]

DESCENDANTS OF DANIEL PRINCE.

I. "First Generation."—**Daniel¹ Prince** was born in Birmingham, Old England, May 1st, 1755. He joined the British army and came to this country in 1777 under General Burgoyne, and was probably with him in his contemplated grand march through Canada and Eastern New York to the sea, which was brought to an inglorious end by his surrender to General Gates, at Saratoga, Oct. 17, 1777. Burgoyne and his army were sent across the country to Boston as prisoners of war. In passing through Massachusetts, many of the British fell out by the way, and subsequently became American citizens. Mr. Prince was one of this number, and took up his residence in Williamsburg, Mass. In 1779 he married Mary Packard, of Goshen, Mass. She was the daughter of James Packard, one of the first settlers of Goshen, and was a native of Bridgewater, in this state. Mr. Prince died in Springfield, Mass., April 23, 1828. His wife died May 21, 1816. Their remains now rest in the cemetery at Springfield, Mass. They had the following eight children—three sons and five daughters:

NOTE.—The above was furnished in printed form by one of the Descendants, and the Compiler cannot vouch for its authenticity, but believes it to be authentic and reliable.

II. Children of Daniel[1] and Mary (Packard) Prince:

    1 Mehitable, b. J—— 5th, 1780, in Williamsburg, Mass.
    2 Polly, b. June—, 1782, in Williamsburg, Mass.
    3-4 Daniel and James, (twins), b. Dec. 22, 1784.
    5 Sally, b. May—, d. Mar. 13, 1823.
    6 Nancy, b. J—— 1, 1789, d. Dec. 28, 1883.
    7 Ephraim, b. Feb. 11, 1792, d. July—.
    8 Betsey, b. Mar. 13, 1794, d. Feb. 23, 1890.

NOTE.—Above children all born in Williamsburg, Mass. Daniel, one of twins, died Dec. 27, 1876.

II. 4 (3rd ch.) **Daniel**[2] (one of twins, *Daniel*[1]), born in Williamsburg, Mass., Dec. 22, 1784; married Sarah Popkins, of Boston, Mass., in 1807. He died Dec. 27, 1876, aged 92 years, 5 days. His wife died Jan. 18, 1865. Their remains now rest in the cemetery at Agawam, Mass. Mr. Prince at fifteen years of age entered the Armory at Springfield, Mass., as an apprentice, and worked his way up to the position of inspector. He purchased, in 1827, the farm at Agawam, Mass., where he resided, but continued his labors in the Armory until 1835.

III. Children of Daniel and Sarah (Popkins) Prince:

    9 Emily, b. Sept. 8, 1808, d. Dec. 15, 1884.
    10 Sarah, b. June 15, 1810, d. July 1, 1810.
    11 Sarah Ann, b. Apr. 24, 1812, d. Aug. 22, 1813.
    12 Elizabeth, b. May 26, 1814. Never married.
    13 Mary Packard, b. May 1, 1816, d. Mar. 8, 1859.
    14 Daniel, b. Apr. 25, 1818, d. Oct. 27, 1893 or 1883.
    15 Luke Packard, b. May 21, 1820, d. Sept. 18, 1853.
    16 James, b. Sept. 3, 1822, d. Oct. 18, 1883.
    17 Hannah Barker, b. Apr. 14, 1825. P. O. address, Springfield, Mass.
    18 Ephraim, b. Nov. 22, 1827. Never married.
    19 Charles, b. Sept. 2, 1830. P. O. address, Springfield, Mass.

NOTE.—Ephraim and Elizabeth Prince (unmarried) live together on the Old Homestead where their father died, at Springfield, Mass., which is their present P. O. address.

II. 4 (3rd ch.) **James**[2] (one of twins, *Daniel*[1]) born in Williamsburg, Mass., Dec. 22, 1784; died Feb. 19, 1878, in Goshen, Mass., aged 93 years, 2 months; married first about 1806, Elizabeth Hunt, of Cummington; she lived four years and had one child. Mr. Prince went to Hatfield, Mass., where he entered the employ of Dea. Partridge, as a farmer. He entered the Armory to labor in 1810; he engaged in teaming for the government in 1812, and removed to Cummington, Mass., in 1821, where he engaged in farming. He afterwards resided in Goshen, Mass. He married second, Mar. 14, 1811, Sarah Ellis Daily, of Worthington, Mass., born Aug. 8, 1791, in Hatfield, Mass. They had seven children—two sons and five daughters. His wife died Feb. 17, 1855, aged 64 years. Their remains now rest in the cemetery at Chesterfield, Mass.

III. Children by first wife:

20 Sarah Maria, b. in May, 1807, in New Haven, Conn. She married Justus Wright, of Haydenville, and they had two sons, named James and Joseph, both now living, (1896).

III. Children by second wife:

21 Henry James, b. Aug. 16, 1812, Springfield, Mass.
22 Elizabeth, b. Mar. 2, 1815, Springfield, Mass.
23 Anna, b. June 30, 1817,   "   "
24 Abiah, b. Sept. 1, 1819,   "   "
25 Joseph. It was said he was still born in Cummington, Mass., 1826.
26 Lovina, b. Apr. 4, 1833, in Cummington, Mass.

NOTE.—The twins, when in their 93rd year, retained their mental and physical faculties to a remarkable degree; had always enjoyed good health, and retained a vivid memory of the past.

"O, Time and Change! with hair as grey
As was our Sire's in bye-gone day.
How strange it seems with so much gone
Of life and love, to still live on!
Yet Love will dream and Faith will trust
That somehow, somewhere, meet we must."

8   DESCENDANTS OF DANIEL PRINCE.

III. 21 (2nd ch.) **Henry³ James** *(James² , Daniel¹)*, born in Springfield, Mass., Aug. 16, 1812; married in Enfield, Conn., Oct. 15, 1834, by Mr. Kingsbury, Lovina Pelton, born in Northampton, Mass., Oct. 23, 1816, and was a daughter of Tracy and Merinda Pelton. Mr. Prince died in Warren, Mass., May 11, 1895, aged 82 years, 9 months, 25 days. She is now living (1895) with her daughter, Sarah, in Worcester, Mass., No. 7 Burncoat St.

IV.   Children:
- 27 Mary Louisa, b. Feb. 2, 1841, Windsor, Mass; d. July 6, 1877.
- 28 Franklin Tracy, b. Aug. 28, 1843, Dalton, "
- 29 Lewis Edgar, b. Dec. 11, 1845, in Northampton, Mass.
- 30 Ella Lovina, b. Feb. 9, 1849, in Northampton, Mass.; d. May 26, 1880.
- 31 Jane Maria, b. Jan. 24, 1853, in Williamsburg, Mass.
- 32 Sarah Alice, b. July 4, 1856, in Williamsburg, Mass.

P. O. address of children living:

Franklin Tracy Prince, Dorchester, Mass.
Lewis Edgar Prince, Wallaston,   "
Jane Maria (Mrs. John J. Lycett), Warren, Mass.
Sarah Alice (Mrs. C. H. Smith), No. 7 Burncoat St., Worcester, Mass.

III. 22 (3rd ch.) **Elizabeth³** *(James² , Daniel¹)*, born in Springfield, Mass., Mar. 2, 1815; died July 24, 1891, aged 76 years, 4 months; married Josiah Miller.

IV.   Children:
- 33 Harriett, b. Mar.—, 1835; m. first, Addis Gillett, 1852; m. second, Marcus West, 1873; she died Dec.—, 1875; one child by each husband.

34 Eliza Ann, b. Mar.—, 1836; m. Aquilla Moore, 1855; now living in Cheshire, Conn. No children—adopted one of her Sister Harriett's.
35 John, b. Feb.—, 1838; m. Louisa Rice, 1870; d. Aug.—, 1886. They had six children; all living.
36 Celia Maria, b. Nov.—, 1841; d. Nov.—, 1878.
37 Sarah, b. Oct.—, 1843; m. Dwight Thayer, 1869; she d. July—, 1880; had one child.
38 Josiah, b. Oct.—, 1845; d. Sept.—, 1850.
39 William Henry, b. Oct.—, 1847; d. Aug.—, 1872.
40 Amanda, b. July—, 1850; m. Elihu Boice, 1867; she d. Dec.—, 1869; had one child.

P. O. address (1896):

Eliza Ann (Mrs. A. Moore), Cheshire, Conn.

III. 23 Anna[3] (*James*[2], *Daniel*[1]), born in Springfield, Mass., June 30, 1817; died June 23, 1896, in West Chesterfield, Mass., aged 79 years, lacking 7 days; married Jan. 1, 1837, Orrin Rogers; he was born Oct. 7, 1811; died Oct. 22, 1876, aged 65 years, 15 days.

IV. Children:
41 Jane M., b. Mar. 28, 1838.
42 Levi H., b. May 8, 1841.
43 Julia Ann, b. July 1, 1848; d. Feb. 20, 1868, aged 19 years, 8 months.

P. O. address (1896):

Levi H. Rogers, East Charlemont, Mass.
Jane M. (Mrs. Lewis Thayer), West Chesterfield, Mass.

III. 24 Abiah³ (*James²*, *Daniel¹*), born in Springfield, Mass., Sept. 1, 1819; died Jan. 22, 1893, aged 73 years; married,———, Samuel Porter; had six children—two boys and four girls.

III. 26 Lovina³ (*James²*, *Daniel¹*), born in Cummington, Mass., Apr. 4, 1833; married,———, Thomas Buck; is still living; had three sons and one daughter; all living. P. O. address: Williamsburg, Mass.

IV. 27 (1st ch.) **Mary⁴ Louisa** (*Henry³*, *James²*, *Daniel¹*), born in Windsor, Mass., Feb. 2, 1841; married, Oct. 8, 1859, Henry Rice, of Williamsburg, Mass.; she died July 6, 1877, aged 36 years, 5 months, 4 days.

V. Children.

44 Carrie L. Rice, b. Aug. 23, 1859 or 1860.
45 Willard A.   " b. Jan. 10, 1862.
46 Frederick W.   " b. Aug. 14, 1865.
47 Eugene H.   " b. Apr. 9, 1868.
48 Carrie J.   " b. Apr. 22, 1870.
49 Charles L.   " b. Nov. 2, 1872.
50 Frank T.   " b. July 6, 1876.

IV. 28 (2nd ch.) **Franklin⁴ Tracy** (*Henry³*, *James²*, *Daniel¹*), born in Dalton, Mass., Aug. 28, 1843; married, first,———, Nov. 26, 1867; married, second, Jan. 18, 1894, in Dorchester, Mass., Mrs. Laura L. Stebbins, daughter of Wm. G. Stephenson, of Dorchester, Mass.

IV. 29 (3rd ch.) **Lewis⁴ Edgar** (*Henry³*, *James²*, *Daniel¹*), born in Northampton, Mass., Dec. 11, 1845; married July 3, 1870, Sarah R. Stephenson.

V. Children:

51 Florence L., b. Aug. 18, 1871.

52 Harry W., b. July 24, 1876; d. Sept. 14, 1882.
53 Edgar L., b. Oct. 3, 1877.
54 Ernest E., b. July 14, 1882.

NOTE.—Florence L. married Sept.—, 1891.

P. O. address of above family (1896): Wallaston, Mass.

IV. 30 (4th ch.) **Ella⁴ Lovina** *(Henry³, James², Daniel¹)*, born in Northampton, Mass., Feb. 9, 1849; married, June 4, 1867, Lerant Phelps, of Hatfield, Mass., born,——; she died May 26, 1880, aged 31 years, 3 months, 17 days. Children.

IV. 31 (5th ch.) **Jane⁴ Maria** *(Henry³, James², Daniel¹)*, born in Williamsburg, Mass., Jan. 24, 1853; married, June 27, 1872, John J. Lycett, who was born in Warren, Mass.,——. P. O. address (1896): Warren, Mass. Children.

IV. 32 (6th ch.) **Sarah⁴ Alice** *(Henry³, James², Daniel¹)*, born in Williamsburg, Mass., July 4, 1856; married in Worcester, Mass., by Rev. Alonzo Sanderson, (Methodist), Aug. 17, 1876, Charles Henry Smith, who was born in Millbury, Mass., Aug. 31, 1855. P. O. address—1896—: No. 7 Burncoat St., Worcester, Mass.

V. Children:
  55 Ada May Smith, b. Oct. 17, 1884, in Worcester, Mass.

IV. 41 (1st ch.) **Jane⁴ M. Rogers** *(Anna³, James², Daniel¹)*, born Mar. 28, 1838; married Nov. 27, 1853, Lewis Thayer; he was born Dec. 22, 1833. Present P. O. address: West Chesterfield, Mass.

V. Children:
  56 Levi L. Thayer, b. July 9, 1860; d. Nov. 17, 1868, aged 8 years, 4 months.
  57 Clifford M. Thayer, b. Dec. 15, 1865; m. Apr. 30, 1891, Hattie S. Dowes, of Cummington, Mass.; had son, Leon Dowes Thayer, b. Dec. 4, 1895.

P. O. address: Cummington, Mass.

Genealogy of Robert Prince,

of Salem, Mass.,

AS COMPILED BY F. A. PRINCE, WITH A FEW EXTRACTS TAKEN FROM "SOME MATERIAL FOR A GENEALOGY," BY E. PUTNAM, FROM "HISTORICAL COLLECTIONS OF ESSEX INSTITUTE," VOL. XXVII.

It is merely conjecture that Richard and Robert Prince were brothers, yet such may be the case. It has also been supposed that Rebecca Prince, who married Capt. John Putnam, the next door neighbor of Robert Prince, may have been a sister of Robert. This is more than probable from evidence in possession of the writer. She was called "step-daughter" of John Gedney, which serves to still more complicate the family relations in this case.

I. ROBERT PRINCE, b.   ; died at Salem village, now Danvers, Mass., June 4, 1674; will dated May 24, 1674; proved June 30, 1674. Mentions sons, James and Joseph. Daughter, Elizabeth. Wife, Sarah, to be executrix. Thomas and John Putnam, overseers. Robert married April 5, 1662, Sarah Warren of Watertown;   ; she died in jail, May 1692. She married second, Alexander Osborne, an Irishman, whose conduct in attempting to hold the property occupied by his wife after her sons became of age, is not to his credit. A lawsuit was needed before the

ROBERT PRINCE HOUSE,
DANVERS, MASS.
BUILT IN 1669, BY ROBERT PRINCE. THE HOME OF SARAH OSBORN.
PHOTO, TAKEN IN 1895.

property was recovered. Sarah Osborne was accused of being a witch by the "afflicted girls." Her second marriage was unhappy and so depressed her that her mind, dwelling upon that and her changed fortunes, became unbalanced, and on the 29th of February warrants were duly issued for her arrest. She was convicted and sentenced to death, was committed to prison and heavily chained. Frail in body and feeble in mind she yet had strength enough to maintain her innocence of the charge made against her, and from March 7th to May 10th she languished in Boston jail, when death, more considerate than man, released her from her bonds. She was a woman of excellent character, only marred by the fact of her marriage with a man whom she had hired to carry on the place. The gossip excited by this act told against her at the trial.

The house built by Robert Prince is still standing (see illustration) with many changes, on Spring avenue, now Danvers, Mass., formerly Salem village. It is owned by St. John Roman Catholic college and is used as a farm house. It remained in the Prince family until 1800. The original grant was that made to William Pester, but was afterward the property of Capt. William Trask who sold to Robert Prince in 1659. This grant contained about 150 acres, and lay, all of it, westerly of Summer street and northerly from what is now Maple street, over toward the Newburyport turnpike. Robert Prince also owned land on the westerly side of Ipswich river.

For further information concerning Robert Prince, his grant, and his widow, Sarah Osborne, the reader is referred to the work of Hon. C. W. Upham, or "Salem Witchcraft in Outline," by Mrs. C. E. Upham.

Children.

2. James, b. Jan. 19, 1664-5; d. Sept. 1666.
3. James, b. Aug. 15, 1668.
4. Elizabeth, b. Feb. 19, 1669-70.
5. Joseph.

II. JAMES (3), b. in Salem village, Aug. 15, 1668; d. 1724; m. previous to 1693, Sarah Rea, widow of Jacob Phillips, by whom she had a daughter, Silence Phillips, baptized at same time as her mother, Sept. 17, 1693, and who married Dr. Amos Putnam, of Danvers. James Prince was a farmer and lived on the homestead. In the division of their father's estate, James had the eastern and Joseph the western part. The dividing line was Beaver brook, which enters a larger brook, called Whipple's brook, near where is now the house of Mr. Guilford, on Nichols street. The will of James Prince was proved April 3, 1724. All of the real estate was given to sons James and David. Jonathan received £100; to daughters, Charity, Sarah Reding and Rebecca, £40 each; James had the homestead and orchard in front. In 1720 James and Joseph Prince had joined in deeding to their sons, David and Robert, a forty-acre farm near Ipswich river, which had belonged to their father, and the title of which was in controversy at the time James made his will, Aug. 20, 1723.

Children.

6. Sarah, bapt. Apr. 17, 1694; m. Sept. 26, 1717, Thomas Reddin.
7. Charity, bapt. about 1694; m. Mar. 20, 1722, Solomon Town.
8. Rebecca, bapt. Dec. 11, 1698; m. Dec. 25, 1727, Robert Ganfield.
9. James, bapt. Jan. 12, 1700.
10. David, bapt. Jan. 31, 1702.
11. Jonathan, bapt. July 20, 1707.

II. JOSEPH (5), b. in Salem village; m. June 3, 1698, Elizabeth Robinson, who was bapt. July 9, 1704. Joseph had the western part of his father's farm in the division made May 21, 1696.

Children.

12. Robert, b. Dec. 29, 1700; bapt. Oct. 22, 1704.
13. Timothy, b. May 30, 1702; d. y.

14. Joseph, b. Oct. 1703; d. six weeks later.
15. Joseph, bapt. Oct. 22, 1704.
16. Elizabeth, bapt. July 29, 1705; d. y.
17. Solomon, bapt. Mar. 30, 1707. Removed to Salem then to Thompson, Conn. Was a "cordwainer."
18. Susanna, bapt. July 3, 1709.
19. Abel, bapt. Apr. 8, 1711; m. at Salem, July 31, 1735, Hannah Eaton.
20. Martha, bapt. June 21, 1713. Perhaps the Martha who m. 22 Dec., 1747, Thomas Nichols.
21. Elizabeth, bapt. Mar. 18, 1716; m. Oct. 2, 1736, John Nichols.
22. William, bapt. Sept. 8, 1717.
23. Samuel, bapt. June 17, 1719.
24. Timothy, bapt. Aug. 12, 1722.

III. JAMES (9), b. in Salem village; bapt. Jan. 12, 1700; m. Dec. 2, 1730, Hannah, daughter of John (John John) and Hannah Putnam, b. May 7, 1707; d. June 19, 1798, (gravestone). He d. in 1775; his will is dated April 1, 1774; proved May 6, 1776. James Prince styled himself a yeoman and lived on the homestead. He was prominent in parish and town affairs, and was first treasurer of Danvers. Both he and his wife are buried in the Prince lot at Beaver brook.

Children.

25. James, b. Sept. 15, 1731; bapt. Nov. 7, 1731; d. July 27, 1796, aged 65 years (g. s.).
26. Huldah, b. Feb. 9, 1733-4; bapt. Feb. 24, 1733-4; m. her cousin, Timothy Prince, (24). They removed to Pomfret, Conn.
27. David, b. Nov. 27, 1738; bapt. Dec. 3, 1738; d. Jan. 28, 1796. P. S.: Will proved Mar. 6, 1797. Cordwainer in Danvers.
28. John, b. Jan. 26, 1744; bapt. Jan. 29, 1744; d. Apr. 18, 1744.
29. John, b. Nov. 20, 1745; bapt. Nov. 24, 1745. He sold the homestead to Nathan Pierce in 1800.
30. Amos, b. Feb. 17, 1748; bapt. Feb. 17, 1748.

III. DAVID (10), b. in Salem village; bapt. there Jan. 31, 1702; m. there Dec. 3, 1721, Phebe Fuller. David Prince removed to Sutton and died there.

Children.

31. David, b. in Salem village, Oct. 23, 1725; bapt. there Mar. 20, 1725-6.
32. Sarah, b. in Salem village, Apr. 28, 1727; bapt. there May 5, 1728.
33. Stephen, b. Oct. 4, 1730.
34. John, b. Nov. 27, 1733.

III. DOCTOR JONATHAN (11), b. in Salem village; bapt. there July 20, 1707; m. first, Abigail Rogers, of Billerica; m. second, Mary Porter, daughter of Joseph Porter, administrator on the estate of Mary Prince, widow, intestate, July 12, 1782. He died in Salem village, May 1753. His will was dated May 6, and proved May 28, 1753.

Doctor Jonathan Prince was one of the earliest resident physicians in Danvers, perhaps the first. Judge Holton studied medicine with him. He lived on the westerly side of Hathorne's hill, where now stands a grove of pines, and near the sight of the Peabody barn, burnt in July, 1891. The house was moved about 1845 to the corner of Hobart and Forrest streets, and is still standing.

Child by First Wife.

35. Abigail; mentioned in her father's will.

Children by Second Wife.

36. Jonathan, b. (Jan. 21, town record.) Oct. 1734; bapt. Apr. 11, 1735; m. June 6, 1754, Lydia, sister of Judge Holton; d. Dec. 11, 1759, in his twenty-sixth year, (g. s.); buried in Prince lot. He was a physician and lived in Danvers. No issue.
37. Daniel, b Sept. 12, 1735; bapt. Sept. 16, 1735; m. Elizabeth Rea.
38. Nathan, b. June 21, 1738; bapt. June 25, 1738; d. Nov. 22, 1759, aged 22, (g. s.); buried in Prince lot. No issue.

39. Ezra, b. Nov. 9, 1741; bapt. Nov. 22, 1741; m. May 1, 1770, Emma Goodale, of Danvers. Was a cooper. His will was dated Aug. 17; proved Oct. 7, 1771, and mentions wife, "Anne," also his brothers and sisters.
40. Mary, b, May 27, 1744; d. unm., April 26, 1766, (g. s.).
41. Captain Asa, b. Feb. 22, 1746-7; bapt. Feb. 22, 1746-7; m. June 15, 1769, Elizabeth Nichols.
    Note: See F. A. Prince's "War Records of Our Ancestors."
42. Sarah, b. July 13, 1749; bapt. July 23, 1749.
43. Ruth, b. July 28, 1751; bapt. Aug. 4, 1751.

III. ROBERT (12), son of Joseph and Elizabeth (Robinson) Prince, b. in Salem village, Dec. 29, 1700; bapt. Oct. 22, 1704; m. first, Phebe Symonds; m. second, previous to 1747, Mary ———. July 22, 1720, he received his father's share in a forty-acre farm near Ipswich river. In 1747 he sold all his land in Danvers and Middleton to James Jeffrey. He then removed with his family to Killingly, Conn., (North Parish) which is now Thompson. Book 5 of Killingly Land Records contains records of deeds from 1745 to 1754. Page 114 gives the original land purchase of Robert Prince.

I, John Ruwee, have received to my full satisfaction, 1000 pounds, in bills of credit, of Robert Prince, of Salem, in the County of Essex, in the Province of the Massachusetts Bay, in New England, for a certain tract of land, bounded and described as follows, containing by estimation 100 acres, be the same more or less, &c., &c., &c. Signed, sealed and delivered this 7th day of April, in the 21st year of the reign of our Sovereign Lord George the second of Great Britain, Anno Domini 1748.

In Presence of } { Recorded April 7th, 1748.
  Solomon Prince, } {   Joseph Cady,
  Joseph Cady. } {   Town Clerk.

Also in same book, page 115, find that he bought 200 acres of Job Ruwee, for 200 pounds, in bills of credit, at the time he bought the above, and which, it is believed, joined so that it made a farm of 300 acres. Recorded by Joseph Cady, Town Clerk. In presence of Solomon Prince and Joseph Cady.

Larned's History of Windham County, Vol. 1, page 534, says: "Robert Prince, the same year, (1752) bought land east side of the same river, (French or Stony river) of John Stone."

Killingly Land Records, years 1754 to 1759, contain the following deeds in book 6, page 63:

Levi Sylvester sold to Robert Prince for 750 pounds, in bills of credit, of the old tenor, a piece of land containing by estimation 22 acres, be the same more or less, with dwelling house and barn standing thereon, beginning at a white tree, standing on side hill of John Stone's farm, and near Nathaniel Crosby's line, &c., &c. Signed, sealed and delivered this 14th day of March, in the 28th year of the reign of our Sovereign Lord, George the Second. Anno Domini 1755.

Also in same book, page 66, is:—John Stone sold a piece of land, containing by estimation 4 acres, more or less, for 18 pounds, in bills of credit, of the old tenor, paid by Robert Prince, and was at the north-west corner bound of John Stone's farm, and south-west corner bound of Levi White's land. Signed, sealed and delivered this 10th day of January, 1755, and in the 28th year of his reign, George the Second.

In Presence of: { David Prince, Jacob Dresser.

Note: In Killingly, at a Town meeting legally called, on the first Tuesday of December, 1757, "Voted," that Joseph Haskell, Robert Prince and Captain Michael Adams, be a committee on the road from Asa Converse's and Joseph————, toward Thompson meeting house, and make a report at an adjourned meeting.

Book 7, Killingly Records, covering years 1759 to 1768, find deed thus:—I, Robert Prince, do sell and confirm unto Joseph Prince and unto his heirs, &c., forever, a certain tract of land, containing by estimation 50 acres, be the same more or less, and that I have received to my full satisfaction, 66 pounds, 14 shillings and 4 pence for the same. The land is bounded and described as follows: Beginning at a white-oak staddle in corner of the land of the heirs of Isaac Bowen, thence northerly on line of P. Bason Stone's line, thence easterly bordering on line of P. Stone's line, westerly to a fordway in a river, called Stony river, &c., &c. Signed, sealed and delivered this 18th day of November, 1757.

In presence of: Solomon Prince.

Book 8, Killingly Records, 1768 to 1772, page 65, find thus:—I, Robert Prince, for and in consideration of the love and good will and affection I have and do bear toward my son, Ebenezer Prince, have given, granted, and do by these presents freely, fully and absolutely give and grant unto him and his heirs forever, a tract of land, containing by estimation 60 acres. Land formerly belonged to William Richard. Bounded easterly to Nathaniel Crosby's northwest corner bound, &c., &c. Signed, sealed and delivered this 26th day of February, 1768.

In Presence of: { Solomon Ormsbee, Mary (her x mark) Ormsbee.

This Mary was daughter of Robert.

Note: For a more complete and detailed record of the above deeds, consult Killingly Land Records, books 5, 6, 7, 8, at Town Clerk's office, Danielson, Conn.

Children by First Wife.

44. Joseph, bapt. July 19, 1730; m. first, —— Perry; m. second, Elizabeth Starr.
45. Mary, bapt. Apr. 31, 1731; m. Solomon Ormsbee.
46. Ebenezer, bapt. July 3, 1732; m. Rebecca Carroll.
47. Sarah, bapt. July 25, 1736; Probably died young.
48. David, bapt. Feb. 19, 1737; m. Eunice Porter.
49. Sarah, bapt. June 29, 1740; m. William Whittemore.
50. Elizabeth, bapt. Mar. 13, 1742-3; m. Elijah Corbin.

Above born in Salem village.

Children by Second Wife.

51. Susannah, b. in Killingly, (North Parish) now Thompson; bapt. Nov. 13, 1748; m. Mark Dodge.
52. Robert, b. Jan. 20, 1754; m. Jemima Bixby.

Note: Many Danvers families removed to Windham County, Connecticut, during the first half of the Eighteenth century, the above family coming with others, and settled in Pomfret, Thompson, Brooklyn and Killingly.

III. JOSEPH (15), b. in Salem village; bapt. there Oct. 22, 1704; m. about 1749, Elizabeth Rollins, of Souhegan West, (Amherst) N. H. He died in Amherst, Nov. 28, 1789. Joseph Prince is said by the Historian of Amherst to have been one of the proprietors of Narragansett, No. 3, in the right of his uncle, Richard Prince. The only Richard Prince who served in the Narragansett campaign was Richard, son of Richard of Salem, who may have been his father's cousin.

There is some room for doubt concerning the Prince pedigree as given in the History of Amherst.

Children Born at Amherst.

53. Elizabeth, b. Feb. 13, 1750; m. first, David Cady; m. second, Benjamin Roby; d. in Merrimack, Oct. 1830.
54. Joseph, m. Dec. 6, 1775, in Danvers, Sarah Wyatt, of Danvers.
55. Hannah, m. John Hartshorn; d. in Amherst, Dec. 19, 1795, aged 42 years.
56. Sarah, m. Thaddeus Duncklee. They removed to Johnson and afterward to Rutland, Vt.
57. Abel, b. June 1, 1757; m. Nov. 3, 1782, Fanny Cowen; lived in Amherst; d. June 9, 1838. Abel Prince served in the Revolutionary War. (See F. A. Prince's "War Records.")
58. Mary, b. 1760; m. David Melvin; d. Sept. 6, 1844, in Amherst.
59. Susannah, m. Ralph Ellenwood; d. Nov. 10, 1838, in Johnson, Vt., aged 75 years.

60. John, m. Mindwell Mills. They removed to Johnson, Vt. He was in the War of 1812. Died in Indiana.
61. Anna, m. May 5, 1786, David Reddington. Lived in Vermont and Greensborough, Ind.
62. Solomon, b. Aug 4, 1771; m. Jan. 21, 1796, Mary, dau. of Dr. John Mussey. He was a farmer in Amherst. He died Dec. 3, 1863. (Children.)

Note: For further particulars of this family see History of Amherst, N. H., by Daniel F. Secomb.

III. SOLOMON (17), b. 1707; bapt. Mar. 30, 1707. Removed to Salem, and thence to North Parish, of Killingly, (now Thompson). Lived at the present North Grosvenor Dale, in Thompson, Windham Co., Conn., near his brother Robert. He was a "cordwainer." He died Feb. 1767.

Note: In the Spring of 1894, the skeleton and gravestone were unearthed in digging a cellar at above place, for the new house of Samuel Stone, Esq. Solomon was buried in a private lot, it is supposed, by the side of his brother Robert.

Following is an Inventory of Solomon Prince, "deceased estate," as found on page 65, Book 1764 to 1778, of Pomfret, Conn., Probate Records:

An Inventory of the Estate of Solomon Prince, deceased, as appraised by Solomon Ormsbee and Stephen Crosby.

Is a Bed and Bedding,	£2	10s.
Is a Hatt,		15
Is a Hoe and Ax,		17
2 Books,		6
2 Noats and Cash,	199	2
Is a Pot and Kettle, Hammer, Pincers, and 2 pairs Gloves,		12
Total, Mar. ye 10th, 1767,	£210.	

Solomon Ormsbee, } Appraisers Under Oath.
Stephen Crosby,

April 7th, 1767.

III. ABEL (19), bapt. in Salem village, Apr. 8, 1711; m. July 31, 1735, Hannah Eaton.

Children.

63. Elizabeth, bapt. June 8, 1740.
64. Anna, bapt. June 8, 1740; m. John Goodale, of Danvers; published Mar. 15, 1760.
65. Hannah, bapt. Aug. 26, 1741.

III. WILLIAM (22), 11th child of Joseph and Elizabeth (Robinson) Prince, b. in Salem village; bapt. there Sept. 8, 1717. Removed to Pomfret, Conn., near his other brothers, where he married Mary Holland, dau. of Joseph and Elizabeth Holland. He lived in Pomfret (that part which is now Brooklyn) until after 1757, as he was until this date one of the Mortlake Society of this place. (This old Mortlake Society's records commence in the year 1731, and are in the possession of Charles G. Williams, of Brooklyn.) On Sept. 29, 1755, William Prince was chosen society collector for Mortlake Society, and June 10, 1756, was elected member of Pomfret Library. On Jan. 6, 1757, William Prince was chosen one of the committee to take care of the school money. Soon after this, between 1757 and 1760, he moved to what was called the North Parish of New London, now Montville, Conn. His wife, Mary, united with the Congregational Church there, under the pastorate of the Rev. David Jewett, about 1765. She died there April 18, 1799, aged 77 years. Inscription on gravestone: "Mary Williams, whose first husband was William Prince, died April 18, 1799, aged 77 years, 4 months." William Prince died there (Montville) Feb. 21, 1773, in the 56th year of his age; buried in old churchyard on Raymond Hill, Montville. After the death of William Prince, Feb. 21, 1773, his widow (Mary) soon after married, second, Rev. David Jewett, who had been pastor at the above place for a number of years. Jewett's first wife, "Patience," died Nov. 14, 1773. He died June 6, 1783.

There is no record of the marriage of the Rev. David Jewett to his second wife. Soon after Rev. Mr. Jewett's death, his widow, Mary (Holland) (Prince) Jewett, married, third, Mar. 17, 1785, William Williams. She died as above stated, and was buried beside of her first husband, William Prince, in Raymond Hill cemetery, Montville, Ct. William Prince was a large landholder in Montville, and at one time owned the farm on which Captain Jerome W. Williams now lives (1896). He became greatly entangled by debt and was obliged to make an assignment of his property, which left him much impoverished at his death. Elizabeth Holland, the mother of Mary, (his wife) died at Montville, Aug. 23, 1762, aged 64 years. Joseph, the father, died Nov. 18, 1762, in the 68th year of his age. Both were members of the Jewett Church.

Children.

66. Joseph, b. Apr. 25, 1748; d.
67. Eunice, b. Jan. 3, 1750; d.
68. William, b. Mar. 6, 1753; d.   ; lived in Montville, Conn.
69. Luce, b. Oct. 21, 1755; d.
70. Elizabeth, b. Mar. 12, 1760, in Montville.

Note: First four children born in Pomfret, as found in Pomfret records.

The history of the Raymond family (Henry A. Baker) contains the following:

"Joshua Raymond, b. about 1753; m. first, Mary Raymond, who died the first year of their marriage without issue. He then m. Elizabeth Prince, b. Mar. 12, 1760, dau. of William Prince and (Mary Holland). They had ten children: seven daughters and three sons. Elizabeth died Jan. 2, 1844, at Montville, aged 83 years, 9 months, 20 days."

III. TIMOTHY (24), b. in Salem village; bapt. Aug. 12, 1722; d. in Brooklyn, Conn., July 6, 1798, in the 77th year of his age, (g. s.). He m. first, 1744, Mary, dau. of Joshua and Rachel (Goodale) Putnam. She was b. June 26, 1727; d. Dec. 17, 1754. He m. second, Oct. 15, 1755, his cousin, Huldah Prince, (26) dau. of James and Hannah (Putnam) Prince. She (Huldah) died in Brooklyn, Conn., Nov. 29, 1801, in the 69th year of her age, (g. s.).

Children by First Wife.

71. Samuel, b. Nov. 9, 1745; bapt. May 31, 1747, in Salem village.
72. Phebe, b. Dec. 9, 1748; bapt. Dec. 18, 1748, in Salem village; d. May 23, 1750.
73. Betty, b. Dec. 17, 1751; bapt. Dec. 22, 1751, in Salem village.

Children by Second Wife.

74. Timothy, b. Nov. 3, 1756; bapt. Nov. 7, 1756, in Danvers, Mass.; d. in Brooklyn, Conn., May 31, 1809, (g. s.).
75. Hannah, b. Oct. 3, 1760; bapt. Oct. 19, 1760, in Danvers.
76. Abel (Capt.), b. in Pomfret, Conn., July 3-5, 1763; d. in Brooklyn, Conn., Jan. 17, 1819, (g. s.). Note: Town Record says b. 5th; g. s. says b. 3d July. Married Lucy Cady, dau. of Uriah Cady, of Brooklyn. She d. April 21, 1842, in Brooklyn; age 77 years, (g. s.)

March 26, 1746, William and Timothy Prince sold to Joshua Putnam, land in Middleton, and Dec. 9, 1757, Timothy Prince, with consent of his wife, Huldah, sold to George Wiat, of Danvers. A short time after 1760, they removed to Pomfret, Conn., near his other brothers.

Timothy Prince's name appears on Pomfret Probate Records, book 11, page 22; also Maj. Timothy Prince's inventory, page 33-4, same book; also Maj. Timothy's distribution of his real estate, page 393. There is also in book 12, page 302, something concerning John Prince, son of Col. Timothy Prince.

Cannot say whether the above relates to Timothy, Sr., or Timothy, Jr.; probably the latter.

There is also in Brooklyn cemetery, Brooklyn, Conn., a gravestone with the following inscription: "In memory of Mrs. Polly Prince, wife of John Prince, who departed this life Jan. 26, 1808, in the 42nd year of her age." Perhaps she was (Polly Hayward), and that he was John, son of James and Hannah Putnam. See No. 29. Can anyone give me information about this John?

IV. JAMES (25), bapt. in Salem village, Nov. 7, 1731; m. Elizabeth, dau. of Moses (John) Preston, who d. Dec. 18, 1822, aged 86 years, (g. s.). He d. in Danvers, July 27, 1796, aged 65 years. In 1796 he deeded to his sons, Joseph and Caleb, one half his farm, in all fifty-five acres, on Hathorne Hill. In the inventory of his estate, fifty-five acres is mentioned as half of the homestead. Administration was granted on his estate to Joseph, Nov. 10, 1796, who gave bonds with Caleb Prince and Ebenezer Goodale.

Children.

77. Moses, b. Feb. 14, 1756. Served in the Revolution as Lieut. See F. A. Prince's "War Records."
78. Joseph, b. June 27, 1761; m. Betsey————, who d. Mar. 10, 1859, aged 86 years; he d. July 18, (July 17, Town Record) 1840, aged 79 years, 1 month, (g. s.).
79. James, b. Aug. 28, 1763; d. July 24, 1796.
80. Caleb, b. Oct. 18, 1769.
81. Hannah, b. Feb. 2, 1772.
82. Betsey, b. Oct. 24, 1774.
83. Amos, b. Aug. 30, 1776.

IV. STEPHEN (33), b. Oct. 4, 1730, in Salem village; removed with his parents to Sutton, Mass; m. Abigail Perkins, Sept. 16, 1755-6.

Children.

84. Abigail, b. Jan. 4, 1756. (?)
85. Phœbe, b. July 25, 1757; m. Apr. 14, 1779, Daniel Sibley.

86. Sarah, b. Nov. 25, 1758; m. July 20, 1780, Henry Harback.
87. Hannah, b. May 18, 1760; m. Apr. 5, 1781, Eleazer Putney.
88. Mollie, b. Aug. 30, 1763; m. Apr. 6, 1788, Joseph Carriel.
89. Huldah, b. Oct. 25, 1765; m. Oct. 20, 1785, Billy Brown.
90. Miriam, b. May 17, 1767; m. Apr. 26, 1787, Moses Alton, of Charlton, Mass.
91. Jonathan, b. Feb. 1, 1769, in Sutton, Mass.; m. Patty Vinton.
92. David, b. Jan. 1, 1771; m. Apr. 14, 1799, Rebekah Shumway. She was b.—1781; d. Aug. 26, 1876. He d. Sept. 24, 1847.
93. Stephen, b. Nov. 4, 1772; m. Abigail Pratt.
94. Ruth, b. Feb. 8, 1775; m. David Shumway, son of Ebenezer Shumway.
95. Lydia, b. Mar. 8, 1777; m. Nov. 30, 1797, Jennison Twiss, of Charlton, Mass.
96. Naomi, b. May 8, 1781; m. Jan. 16, 1803, David Morse, of Charlton, Mass.

All the above children born in Sutton, Mass. The last five, with their mother, came to Oxford. She died there Nov. 28, 1820, aged 83 years.

IV. DANIEL (37), b. in Salem village, Sept. 12, 1735; m. first, Mar. 15, 1763, Elizabeth Rea; m. second, Anne Felton; such an intention is recorded July 18, 1777, for which a certificate was issued on Aug. 3, 1777. Anne (Felton) Prince was the daughter of Nathaniel and Dorcas (Upton) Felton, of Danvers, Mass.; b. there Nov. 5, 1754; probably removed to Bow, N. H.

Children.

97. Daniel, b.   ; m.
98. Anne, b.   ; m. ——— Cheever, but is said by Mr. Amos Prince to have m. Nathaniel Felton.

IV. CAPT. ASA (41), b. in Salem village, Feb. 22, 1747; m. June 15, 1769, Elizabeth Nichols. He served two days as Capt. in the Lexington alarm, April 19, 1775; also served as Capt. at various other times. See F. A. Prince's "War Records of the Princes," pub. 1898, Danielson, Ct., which gives a very extended account of his services in the Revolutionary war. He was noted for his courage and devotion to his country, and for his coolness in face of danger. He received his commission as Captain in line of promotion.

Children.

99. Jonathan, b. Apr. 29, 1771.
100. Elizabeth, b. Jan. 15, 1774.

IV. JOSEPH (44), son of Robert and Phebe Symonds, was b. in Salem village; bapt. there July 19, 1730; removed with his parents about 1747 to Connecticut; d. in Pomfret, Conn., April 19, 1801; will probated April 29, 1801; m. first, in Thompson, Conn., ———— Perry; m. second, Feb. 4, 1776, by Rev. Noadiah Russell, Elizabeth Starr, dau. of Comfort and Elizabeth Starr, of Thompson, Conn. She was b. Sept. 13, 1734; died Mar. 19, 1822, aged 87 years, 6 months, 6 days.

Children by First Wife.

101. Rachel, bapt. in Thompson, Apr. 6, 1755.
102. Rebecca, bapt. in Thompson, Feb. 1, 1758.
103. Mary, bapt. in Thompson, Apr. 12, 1763.
104. Anna, bapt. in Thompson, Apr. 28, 1765.

(Thompson, Conn., Church Records.)

In his will he calls "Rebecca" his youngest daughter, and only mentions his three daughters. Probably "Anna" died previous to his making the will.

Last Will of the above Joseph Prince, (Robt., Jos., Robt.).

In the name of God, Amen. I, Joseph Prince, of Thompson, in the County of Windham, and State of Connecticut, calling to mind the mortality of my body, and knowing that it is appointed for all men once to die, being of sound mind and memory, blessed be God therefor, do make and ordain this my last will and testament in manner and form following: Principally and first of all I give and recommend my soul into the hand of God who gave it, and my body to the earth to be buried in a Christian burial, and as touching such worldly estate as it hath pleased God to bless me with in this life, I give, demise and bequeath and dispose of in the following manner:

First, I give and bequeath to my beloved wife, Elizabeth Prince, all the household goods and furniture and wearing apparel and books which she brought with her when I married her, and also a pewter platter, a pint pot and two plates which she bought with her money, also all the monies which is due to me on all the notes and obligations as are given to me and Elizabeth Prince. I also give and bequeath to my beloved wife, Elizabeth Prince, one linen bed ticking, one red and white bed blanket, one tow and linen sheet and two pillow cases, three pairs tow sheets, one pair woolen sheets, one of the best table cloths, two pairs napkins, and also one cow, all of which articles for her to dispose of as she may please, and also ten sheep at her disposal, and also I give and bequeath one cow more for her to keep for her own use, and also three of the above said sheep and one of the cows to be kept by my Executor for her to take all the profits of them, she to sell off the lambs in the fall, if any there are, the one sheep and three sheep to be kept for her summer and winter. My real estate, all of my lands and buildings, I give and bequeath to my eldest daughter, Rachel Copeland, to her and her heirs, and I give and bequeath to my second daughter, Mary Bixbee, the sum of one hundred and fifty dollars, the one-half within one year after my decease and the other half within two years after, to be paid by my Executor, hereafter named, and to my youngest daughter, Rebecca Atwood, I give and bequeath the sum of one hundred and fifty dollars, to be paid the one-half within one year after my decease and the other half within two years after, and to the rest and remainder of my estate I give and bequeath as follows, viz.:

One bed and bedding I give to my daughter Rachel, and one bed and bedding I give to my daughter Rebecca, and my household furniture and wearing apparel it is my will to have equally divided among my three daughters, and my stock and all my monies and tools and obligations for money, I give and bequeath to my son-in-law, Phineas Copeland, whom I ordain and constitute and appoint my Executor in this my last will and testament together with Elijah Atwood, both Executors. But Phineas Copeland to have the monies and stock and tools before last mentioned, and the said Phineas Copeland to pay all the aforesaid bequeaths and legacies, and to pay all my just debts and charges of a Christian burial, and I declare that my will is that so long as my wife shall live and continue my widow, Phineas Copeland, who is one of the Executors, and I direct him that he shall take care of and provide for my said wife, Elizabeth, during her widowhood, as follows, viz.: she to have the improvement of the north room in my dwelling house and the chamber over it, and the north-west room and the cellar under it, and the chamber over it, with a privilege of the well and dooryard, the house to be kept in repair suitable for her, and the said Copeland to keep one cow and three sheep for her, and provide and keep a horse for her to ride to meeting and elsewhere as she may have occasion; to provide and find fire wood at her door suitable for her, and provide and find good and suitable provision of all sorts for her, and find her with shoes, in a word provide everything necessary for her, in sickness and health, so long as she remains my widow, and see that she has a decent and Christian burial at death. Hereby revoking all former wills by me made, I declare this to be my last will and testament.

In witness whereof I have hereunto set my hand and seal this 12th day of November, 1799.

JOSEPH (his x mark) PRINCE.

Signed, sealed, published and declared by the above named Joseph Prince to be his last will and testament, in presence of us who have hereunto subscribed our names as witnesses in the presence of the testator.

Windham, ss. Thompson, April 29th, 1801.
{ JASON PHIPPS,
SARAH (her x mark) PHIPPS,
ASENATH PALMER.

Then personally appeared Sarah Phipps and Asenath Palmer and severally made solemn oath that they saw and heard the testator, Mr. Joseph Prince, sign, seal, publish and declare the within written instrument to be and contain his last will and testament, and that at the time he was of sound disposing mind and memory, and subscribed our names thereto as witnesses in the presence of the testator and each other.

Before me, JASON PHIPPS, Justice of the Peace.

At a Court of Probate, held at Pomfret, within and for the District of Pomfret, July 7th, 1801,

Present, THOMAS GROSVENOR, ESQ., Judge.

Personally appeared Phineas Copeland, one of the Executors named in the foregoing will of Mr. Joseph Prince, late of Thompson, deceased, and exhibited the same for probate and accepted the trust reposed in him, and this will being proved, is by this Court approved and ordered to be recorded and kept on file, (the other Executor, Mr. Elijah Atwood, being notified of the time and place of exhibiting the will, did not appear to accept the trust or refuse), the said Copeland, the acting Executor, having given bond in the sum of $2000 for the faithful performance of his trust.

Test., LEMUEL GROSVENOR, Clerk of Probate.

Truly recorded. Test., L. GROSVENOR, Cl'k of Probate. Probate Office, Dist. of Pomfret, May 27th, 1895.

The foregoing is a true copy of Record in this Office.

Attest, L. S. HAYWARD, Judge of Probate for District of Pomfret.

Inventory of Estate of Joseph Prince.

Real Estate, $1676.67. Personal Estate, $239.71.

May 22, 1801.

Estate of Elizabeth Prince, widow of Joseph Prince. Amt. of her Inventory, $313.82. July 2, 1801.

IV. EBENEZER (45), third child of Robert (12) by first wife, Phebe Symonds, probably b. in Salem village, and was bapt. there July 3, 1732. Removed with his parents to Thompson, Conn., and m. there by Rev. Marston Cabot, June 20, 1755, Rebekah Carroll. She was b.   ; d. May 3, 1804, in Thompson, aged 78 years, (g. s.). He d. Oct. 8, 1802, aged 73 years, (g. s.); buried in West Thompson. Thompson held its first town meeting June 21, 1785. The Freeman's Oath was administered to 78 persons, and at this meeting they elected Ebenezer Prince as one of the Highway Surveyors and Collectors of the town. Thompson was formerly a part of Killingly.

Ebenezer Prince, of Killingly, bought of Joseph Ellyot, of Sutton, in County of Worcester, Province of Massachusetts Bay, in New England, for 86 pounds, 13 shillings and 4 pence, lawful money, a tract of land containing 55 acres, with buildings thereon, be the same more or less: Beginning at a white-oak tree, thence westerly, &c., adjoining land of Robert Prince, &c., &c., being near and adjoining Nathaniel Crosby's land, &c. I have hereunto set my hand and seal this 6th day of February, and in the twenty-ninth year of his Majesty's reign. Anno Domini 1756.

In Presence of: { JONATHAN CARRIEL, JOSEPH ELLYOT, JR.

For a more full description of the above deed, refer to book 6, 1754 to 1759, page 113, of Killingly Land Records.

Children.

104.A. John, b.   ; bapt. Feb. 26, 1758; d.
105.   Eunice, b.   ; bapt. Feb. 26, 1758; d.
       ; m. John Foster, Sept. 2, 1804; both of Thompson. Pomfret Probate Records, book 9, 1798, page 617, says that Eunice Foster, late Eunice Prince, appeared at a Court of Probate.
106.   Abel, b.   ; bapt. Nov. 25, 1759; d.   ; m. Mar. 8, 1782, by Rev. Noadiah Russell, Lucy Nichols; children.
107.   Lucy, b.   ; bapt. Feb. 12, 1762; d. Aug., 1844.

Last Will of Ebenezer Prince.

In the name of God, Amen. I, Ebenezer Prince, of Thompson, in the County of Windham, being of sound and disposing mind and memory, blessed be God, do make and ordain this my last will and testament in manner and form following; that is to say:

I will that all my debts and funeral charges be paid and discharged by my Executors, hereinafter named.

Item 1.   I give to my well-beloved wife, Rebecca, one-third part of the farm I now live on, for to use during her natural life, and also the use of all my indoor movables during her life, and also three hundred thirty-three dollars and thirty-four cents, to be paid to her by my said Executors.

Item 2.   I give to my well-beloved son, Abel, all my wearing apparel, the whole of the farm he hath had the possession of, and now leaseth out, and also about 40 acres of land lying south of the pasture, and the same land I bought of Hulet & Jewet.

Item 3. I give to my well-beloved daughter, Eunice Prince, the whole of my home farm I now live on, her mother having her thirds during life, and also all my indoor movables after the death of her mother.

Item 4. I give to my four grand-children—John, Ebenezer, Rebecca and Dyer Town, one hundred and fifty dollars, to be paid by my Executors, to be equally divided between them, and if they should not be of age at the time of my death, my will is, the money be paid by my said Executors to Elijah Crosby, and be by him put out on interest, for the use of the children when they come of age; also I give to my grand-child, Ebenezer Town, my gun and bayonet.

Item 5. I give to the the children of my son Abel, 20 acres of land I bought of John Hewlett. I also give all the rest of my estate, real and personal, to my two children, Abel and Eunice, they paying my debts, legacies and funeral charges, and also ordain the said Abel and Eunice Prince my sole Executors to this my last will and testament.

In witness whereof I have hereunto set my hand and seal, and do publish, pronounce and declare this to be my last will and testament, in the presence of us, who in the presence of each other have subscribed our names as witnesses. Dated at Thompson, May 16th, 1801.

EBEN PRINCE. (L. S.)

ELEAZER MOFFIT,
PHINEAS COPELAND,
POLLY COPELAND.

Windham, ss. Thompson, Nov. 18th, 1802.

Then personally appeared Phineas and Polly Copeland, two of the witnesses to the within will, and made solemn oath that they saw the within named Ebenezer Prince sign and seal the within will, and heard him publish, pronounce and declare the same to be his last will and testament, and that he appeared to us to be at that time of sound mind and memory, and that we, together with Eleazer Moffit, Esq., in the presence of the testator and each other, subscribed our names as witnesses.

Before me, ELEAZER MOFFIT,
Justice of the Peace.

At a Probate Court, held at Pomfret, in the District of Pomfret, Dec. 7th, 1802,

Present, THOMAS GROSVENOR, ESQ., Judge.

Personally appeared Abel and Eunice Prince, Executors to the foregoing will, and accepted the trust reposed in them, and this will being proved, is by this Court approved and allowed of, and ordered to be recorded and kept on file.

Test, LEMUEL GROSVENOR, Clerk of Probate.

Truly recorded. Test, L. GROSVENOR, Cl'k of Probate.

True copy of Record, L. S. HAYWARD,
Judge of Probate.

{ Seal of Probate Court, }
{   Dist. of Pomfret.   }

Note: Pomfret Probate Records, book 9, 1798, page 461, gives the will. Pages 464-5 gives inventory; total, $7128.64.

IV. MARY (45), dau. of Robert (12) and Phebe (Symonds) Prince, b. in Salem village; bapt. there April 31, 1731; m. in Thompson, Conn., Sept. 4, 1759, Solomon Ormsbee—nothing further known other than what is found in Pomfret Probate Records, which gives the amount of his estate to be 230 pounds, 14 shillings, 9 pence. Also there was a Court of Probate held Dec. 7, 1773, giving the appraisal as 388 pounds, 14 shillings, 9 pence. In 1768 Solomon Ormsbee and Mary, his wife, witnessed the will of their father, Robert, which gave to Ebenezer 60 acres.

IV. DAVID (48), was the fifth child, and by first wife of Robert (12); was bapt. Feb. 19, 1737; d.   ; m. Eunice Porter, Dec. 20, 1763, in Thompson, Conn., by Rev. Noadiah Russell. She was the third child of nine children of Samuel and Hannah Porter, and was b. May 12, 1743.

Children.

108. Samuel Porter, b. Nov. 1, 1764; bapt. Aug. 2, 1767; d.
109. Eunice, b. Aug. 26, 1766; bapt. Aug. 2, 1767; d.
110. David, b.   ; bapt. Aug. 28, 1768; d.
111. Alpheus, b.   ; bapt. Apr. 7, 1771; d.
112. William, b.   ; bapt. July 11, 1773; d.
113. Eli, b.   ; bapt. May 7, 1775; d.
114. Jonathan, b.   ; bapt. Jan. 17, 1779; d.

(Above from Thompson and Killingly Records.)

Nothing further is known of this family. Will anyone kindly inform me of their whereabouts, and greatly oblige the compiler?

IV. SARAH (49), probably b. in Salem village; bapt. June 29, 1740; removed with her parents to Thompson, Conn.; m. in Thompson by Rev. Noadiah Russell, Nov. 21, 1758, William Whittemore, who was b.   ; d. Aug. 15, 1810, (g. s. broke.), in his 77th year. She d. Feb. 26, 1820, in her 80th year, (g. s.); buried in West Thompson.

Inscription on Gravestone of their son, Lyman:

"In memory of Mr. Lyman Whittemore, son of Mr. William Whittemore and Mrs. Sarah, his wife. Died Aug. 24th, 1802, in his 18th year.

> Behold my grave as you pass by,
> For as you are, so once was I;
> But as I am, so you must be;
> Prepare for death, and follow me."

Buried by the side of his father and mother at West Thompson.

IV. ELIZABETH (50), probably b. in Salem village; bapt. there March 13, 1742-3; removed with her parents to Thompson, Conn.; m. there Dec. 29, 1765, Elijah Corbin, by Rev. Noadiah Russell.

Children.

115. Elijah, b. June 28, 1767; m. June 23, 1790, Orinda Child.
116. Parley, b. May 22, 1769; m. Dolly Perrin.
117. Daniel, b. Sept. 22, 1771; d.
118. Betty, b. May 31, 1774; d.

Child of Parley and Dolly (Perrin) Corbin.

Schuyler, b.   ; lived in Thompson, northwest of the present Grosvenor Dale, Conn.

Child of Elijah and Orinda (Child) Corbin.

Parley, b. May 5, 1791.

Note: Parley Corbin and his wife, Dolly, are buried in New Boston, Conn. He d. Jan. 8, 1844, aged 74 years, 8 months. Both have headstones at their graves.

IV. SUSANNAH (51), b. in Thompson, Conn.; bapt. there Nov. 13, 1748; m. there by the Rev. Noadiah Russell, Nov. 17, 1768, Mark Dodge, son of Daniel Dodge, of Dudley, Mass. Susannah was the eight child of Robert (12), and first child of second wife.

Page 251, book 8, of Killingly Land Records, we find the deed of Daniel Dodge, of Dudley, in the County of Worcester, and Province of Massachusetts Bay, in New England. In consideration of 40 pounds, lawful money, paid me by my son, Mark Dodge, of Killingly, in the County of Windham, and Colony of Connecticut, (Blacksmith), for 75 acres, by estimation, bounded, &c., as follows: By Capt. Corbin, John Webster, Paul Dudley. Signed, sealed and delivered, 23d of Oct., 1765.

Also in book 10, page 171, of Land Records, we find where Clement Corbin sold a piece of land to Mark Dodge, containing by estimation 3 acres, be the same more or less, for 50 shillings, lawful money, beginning at a stake in S. W. corner in a swamp, which is a S. W. corner of Mark Dodge's land, and is the north line of land of Elijah Corbin, west on land of Clement Corbin, &c.

I have hereunto set my hand and seal this 10th day of May, 1769. CLEMENT CORBIN.

Also we find where Mark and Susannah Dodge sold a tract of land, with buildings standing thereon, to Daniel Mansfield, in the northerly part of Killingly, containing 78 acres more or less. (We conclude it is the 75 and the 3 acres he bought as above).

We have hereunto set our hands and seal this 9th day of May, 1777. MARK DODGE,
SUSANNAH DODGE.

They moved about 1774 from Thompson to Dudley, as the Dudley Records show they had a son born and so recorded May 3, 1774.

Children of Mark and Susannah (Prince) Dodge.

119. Mark, b. Dec. 23, 1769, in north of Killingly, now Thompson; m.
120. David, b. Jan. 5, 1771-2, in north of Killingly, now Thompson; probably d. young.
121. Paul, b. May 3, 1774, in Dudley; m. Rhoda White, of Charlton, Mass.; d. Jan. 1, 1854.

122. Dorcas, b. Oct. 10, 1776, in Dudley; m. William Fisher, Jr., Apr. 3, 1796; d.
123. Susannah, b. Mar. 1780, in Dudley; m. Joshua Davis, Mar. 13, 1799; d.
124. Molly, b. Mar. 31, 1782, in Dudley; m.
125. Thede, b. Mar. 5, 1784, in Dudley; m.   ; d.
126. David, b. Nov. 6, 1786, in Dudley; m. Tamer Wakefield, of Dudley, (the part of Dudley that is now Webster). She was b. Dec. 21, 1790; d. Jan. 1, 1875, aged 84 years, 10 days. David d. Oct. 31, 1861, aged 74 years, 10 months, 25 days, in Dudley.

Of the above children, the first two found on Killingly Records; the other six on Dudley Records.

Children of David (126).

Rufus, b.   in Dudley; m.   ; d. in Cambridge, Mass., May 30, 1890, aged 79 years, 6 months; buried in Charlton, Mass.

Lorain, b.   in Dudley; m.   ; d. in Cambridge, Sept. 8, 1890, aged 76 years and 3 months; buried in Charlton.

David, b. May 3, 1828, in Charlton City, and now lives there on the old Dodge place, (1895); m. Nov. 19, 1856, Carrie C——— Gale, of Charlton; has two married daughters.

IV. ROBERT* (52), b. Jan. 20, 1754, in Killingly (now Thompson) Conn.; was second child by second wife of Robert (12); d. at the home of his son Asa, Jan. 3, 1829, aged 76 years; m. Mar. 17, 1775, in Thompson, Jemima Bixby, who was b. May 2, 1756; d. Sept. 18, 1821, aged 65 years, (g. s.). She was the first of six children of Nathan Bixby, Jr., and Mary Burrill, who were married in 1755. Nathan Bixby, Sr., came from Topsfield, Mass.; united with the church in Thompson, by letter, 1733. Funeral text of Jemima: Isaiah 3:10, "Say ye to the righteous, that it shall be well with him: for they shall eat the

---

* Served in the Revolutionary War. See F. A. Prince's "War Records."

fruit of their doings." Inscription on gravestone: "Oh! if you knew as much as I, you quickly would prepare to die."

Robert and Jemima lived on the old homestead (see illustration) on the hill, about one-half mile east of North Grosvenor Dale, Conn., and were buried in Smith cemetery, near West Thompson station.

Will of Robert Prince (52).

In the name of God, Amen. I, Robert Prince, of Dudley, [Made his will and died at his son, Asa's.—The author.] in the County of Worcester, and Commonwealth of Massachusetts, although laboring under some bodily infirmities at present, yet possessing a sound disposing mind, memory and understanding, and considering that it is appointed unto all men once to die, do make and ordain this my last will and testament. That is to say, first of all I resign my soul to God, who gave it, and my body I desire may be buried in a decent and Christian-like manner, hoping for a blessed immortality through the mercies of my Redeemer, and as to such temporal estate as I have been blessed with, after my just debts and funeral expenses are paid, I give and dispose of in manner and form following, viz:

First, I give and bequeath unto my son, Nathan Prince, eight-twentieth parts of all my estate which I may leave at my decease, except my household furniture, of which I give him one-fourth part.

I give and bequeath unto my son, Lyman Prince, five-twentieth parts of all my estate at my decease, except my household furniture, of which I give him one-fourth part.

I give and bequeath unto my son, Asa Prince, one-twentieth of my estate, except my household furniture, of which I give him one-fourth part, and also I give him a note of hand which I hold against him, of the sum of $500, dated Jan. 3, 1822.

I give and bequeath unto my son, Robert Prince, six-twentieths of my estate, except my household furniture, and I give him up a note of hand which I hold against him, of the sum of $350, dated Jan. 3, 1822.

I give and bequeath unto my daughter, Jemima Benson, wife of Thomas Benson, one-fourth part of my household furniture, and in making the several proportions before mentioned, the two notes are not to be brought into account in the general sum.

Lastly, I do hereby constitute and appoint Jonathan Nichols, of Thompson, sole Executor to this my last will and testament, hereby revoking all former wills by me at any time heretofore made.

In witness whereof I have hereunto set my hand and seal this 13th day of September, A. D. 1828.

ROBERT PRINCE. (L. S.)

Signed, sealed, published and pronounced by the said Robert Prince, the testator aforesaid, who in his presence and in the presence of each other, have hereunto subscribed our names as witnesses thereto.

WILLIAM TOWN,
HORATIO PHELPS,
HAMMOND HEALY.

Windham County, ss. Thompson, Feb. 19, 1829.

Personally appeared before me, William Town and Hammond Healy, and made solemn oath that they attested the written will of Robert Prince and subscribed the same in the presence of the testator, in the presence of the other subscribing witness to said will, and that said testator at the time of the execution thereof was of sound mind and memory, and signed and published said will in the presence of said dependents and the other subscribing witness thereto.

JONATHAN NICHOLS, Justice of the Peace.

LYMAN PRINCE.
PAGE 41. NUMBER 133.

District of Pomfret } ss. Pomfret, July 30, 1858.
Probate Office.

The foregoing is a true copy as appears of record of the last will and testament of Robert Prince, of Dudley, in the County of Worcester, and Commonwealth of Massachusetts.

CHARLES J. GROSVENOR,
Judge of Probate for said District.

Children.

127. Nathan, b. Jan. 25, 1777; d. Apr. 19, 1859, aged 82 years; buried near West Thompson station; m. twice.
128. Not named, b. and d. Jan. 22, 1778.
129. John, b. Apr. 29, 1779; drowned June 12, 1782.
130. John, b. Sept. 19, 1782; probably d. young.
131. Polly, b. Oct. 22, 1784; m. Nov. 3, 1806, John Jacobs; d. Aug. 31, 1846, aged 61 years, 10 months, 9 days.
132. Asa, b. Aug. 21, 1786; m. Nov. 24, 1812; d. Feb. 21, 1861; buried at New Boston.
133. Lyman, b. Sept. 7, 1790; d. Dec. 8, 1877, aged 87 years, 4 months, 1 day; buried at West Thompson. He never married; was a singular and eccentric man; lived and died at the house of his brother Robert.
134. Joshua, b. Dec. 30, 1792; probably d. young.
135. Robert, b. Oct. 5, 1795; m. May 17, 1821, Hannah Phipps; d. Oct. 16, 1866, aged 71 years, 11 days; buried at West Thompson.
136. Jemima, b. Apr. 2, 1797; d. Sept. 25, 1856, aged 57 years; buried at West Thompson, near main entrance.

IV. WILLIAM (68), son of William (22) and Mary (Holland), b. Mar. 6, 1753, in Pomfret, Conn.; d.——1806, in Washington, Ga.; m. May 6, 1775, in Montville, Conn.,

Mary Hillhouse, who was b. Apr. 10, 1753, at New London, Conn., and was the eldest daughter and eighth child of Judge William and Sarah (Griswold) Hillhouse. She d. Apr. 15, 1814, aged 61 years, 5 days, and was buried in Montville. (Montville Records, H. A. Baker.) Judge William Hillhouse was the second son of Rev. James Hillhouse and Mary Fitch, of New London, Conn., North Parish, (now Montville), and was b. Aug. 25, 1728; m. first, Nov.——1750, Sarah Griswold, who was b. at Lyme, Dec. 2, 1728. She was fourth dau. of John Griswold and Hannah Lee.

Above William Prince served from New London, April, 1775, eight days as Sergeant in Capt. Elisha Fox's Company, which went to the relief of Boston in the Lexington alarm. See "Connecticut in the Revolution," page 18, pub. by State of Connecticut. (He removed to Georgia and died Apr. 3, 1806.)—F. W. Prince. Also see "Genealogy of the Hyde Family," 2 Vols., by Reuben H. Walworth, L.L.D., pub. by Joel Munsell, Albany, N. Y., 1864. Also see F. A. Prince's "War Records of Our Ancestors."

Children.

137. William, b. at New London, Conn., May 6, 1776; was graduated from Yale College, 1796; d. 1817, unm. at Savannah, Ga., where he had gone to teach.
138. Sarah, b.   at New London; d. Sept. 26, 1795, aged 16 years. No further particulars.
139. Sarah, b.   ; d. 1817, in Conn. unm.
140. Oliver Hillhouse, b.   1782; m. Mary (Ross Norman.)

IV. SAMUEL (71), was the first of three children of Timothy (24), by his first wife, Mary; he removed from Salem with his parents to Pomfret. Born Nov. 9, 1745, in Salem village; bapt. there May 31, 1747; m. Dec. 5, 1771,

by Rev. Noadiah Russell, Mary Elliott, of Thompson, Conn. She was only dau. of
and was b. July 30, 1752; d. about 1842. At time of marriage he was from Pomfret, Conn. He hung himself. His wife survived him and d. at the home of Orland's son, Horace. Both buried in Charlton, Mass. No gravestones. After Samuel's death, some of the children lived in Thompson, Conn., and some in Dudley, Mass. Samuel lived in Dudley and Charlton.

Children.

141. Thomas, b. Oct. 5, 1772; m. first in Thompson, Conn.; she d. there; m. second, Lydia Williams; d.
142. Huldah, b. May 19, 1774; m. Asa Brackett; d.
143. Polly, b. Aug. 5, 1775; m. Elijah Thompson; d. Mar. 8, 1820.
144. Daniel, b. Mar. 18, 1777; m. Thankful Tourtellotte; d. in Thompson.
145. Rachel, b. Apr. 22, 1778; d. May 7, 1778.
146. Aaron, b. Oct. 27, 1779; m. Sophia Faulkner; d.
147. Willard, b. June 21, 1783; m. first, Annie Stone; d. Apr. 6, 1853, aged 69 years, 8 months, 15 days.
148. Lucy, b. Jan. 30, 1785; is said to have m. ——— Tucker; went West; d.
149. Orland, b. Nov. 14, 1787; m. first, Rebecca Gore; d.
150. Rachel, b. May 26, 1791; m. Calvin Phipps; d.
151. David, b. Oct. 18, 1792; it is said he left home and was never heard from; supposed to have been murdered.
152. Amasa, b. July 14, 1794; m. Mahala Tourtellotte; d.

First six children recorded in Killingly Records.

IV. CAPT. TIMOTHY (72), son of Timothy (24) by his second wife, Huldah, b. in Salem village, Nov. 3, 1756; bapt. there Nov. 7, 1756; moved to Pomfret, Conn., with his parents; m. first, in Pomfret, Dec. 16, 1780, Deidamia Pierce, dau. of   ; she d. about Jan. 31, 1787, ten days after the birth of her last child, (Deidamia), of which she died; m. second, about 1789, Prudence Dennison, dau. of Thomas Dennison; she d. Sept. 12, 1811, aged 49 years, (g. s.) He died   .

Children by First Wife.

153. Lucy, b. Dec. 6, 1781, in Pomfret, Conn.; d. (single) Jan. 27, 1814, of consumption, aged 33 years, (g.s.)
154. Joseph, b. Feb. 17, 1784; m. Henrietta Scarborough, (dau. of Samuel.)
155. Deidamia, b. Jan. 21, 1787; m. Phillip Scarborough.

Children by Second Wife.

156. David, b. May 22, 1791; m. Sophia Ellsworth.
157. Polly, b. Nov. 6, 1794; m William Dennison.
158. John, b. July 2, 1797, in Brooklyn, Conn.; d. about 1841, (single) in Buffalo, N. Y.
159. Betsey, b. Aug. 16, 1801; m. John M. Dennison.

IV. CAPT. ABEL (76), son of Timothy (24) by his second wife, Huldah, b. in Pomfret, Conn., July 3-5, 1763; d. in Brooklyn, Conn., Jan. 17, 1819, (g. s.). (Town Records say he was born July 5th; gravestone says 3rd.) Married Lucy Cady, dau. of Uriah Cady, of Brooklyn; she d. Apr. 21, 1842, aged 77 years, (g. s. in Brooklyn.)

See F. A. Prince's "War Records" for service of Capt. Abel.

Children.

160. Amos, b. May 14, 1788.
161. William, b. July 23, 1791.
162. Uriah Cady, b. June 17, 1795; m. Nancy Allen.
163. Lucy Maria, b. Mar. 13, 1805.

V. JAMES (79), b. in Danvers, Aug. 28, 1763; m. there June 3, 1787, Phebe Parker, who was b. May 21, 1767, in Reading; d. Nov. 12, 1836. He d. there Mar. 3, 1844.

Children.

164. Betsey, b. Aug. 9, 1788; d. at Salem, Apr., 1831.
165. Moses, b. Aug. 18, 1790; d. in Havana, W. I., Aug., 1812.
166. James, b. Mar. 22, 1792; d. June, 1811, at Danvers.
167. Elzaphan, b. Oct. 22, 1794.
168. Nathan, b. Jan. 16, 1797.
169. Joseph, b. Aug. 1, 1799; d. July 27, 1835, at Boston.

V. CALEB (80), b. Oct. 18, 1769, in Danvers; m. Dec. 9, 1798, Anna Cross, who was b. Dec. 6, 1765.

Children.

170. Michael, b. Jan. 1, 1800.
171. Caleb Strong, b. May 30, 1802.

V. AMOS (83), b. Aug. 30, 1776; m. Feb. 3, 1805, Eunice Fuller, who was b. in Danvers, June 17, 1783; d. July 22, 1864. He d. Feb. 24, 1858.

Children.

172. Charlotte, b. June 13, 1805; m. Apr. 13, 1826, Henry Dwinnell, of Danvers; d. Oct. 11, 1847.
173. Ruth Fuller, b. Feb. 14, 1808.
174. Moses, b. June 19, 1809; d. 1884. Mr. Prince is the well-remembered antiquarian. Probably no man ever knew so many of the traditions of his native town and could place so accurately the characters mentioned.
175. Eunice, b. May 19, 1811; m. ——Pope; d. Sept. 30, 1873.
176. Hannah, b. Sept. 14, 1813.
177. Infant, b. and d. Sept. 3, 1815.
178. Elizabeth Preston, b. Jan. 9, 1817.

179. May Jane, b. July 16, 1819.
180. Amos, b. June 1, 1821.
181. James, b. Apr. 4, 1823.

V. JONATHAN (91), son of Stephen and Abigail (Perkins) Prince, was born Feb. 1, 1769, in Sutton, Mass. Married, Feb. 1792, Patty Vinton, of Dudley, Mass. They settled in Dudley, but removed to Oxford, Mass.

Children.

182. Chester, b. June 18, 1792, in Oxford.
183. Lydia, b. Oct. 11, 1793, in Oxford.
184. John, b. Dec. 2, 1795, in Oxford.
185. Chandler, b. June 14, 1797, in Oxford.
186. Dolly, b. Sept. 25, 1799, in Oxford.
187. Juley (Julia), b. Dec. 19, 1809, in Sturbridge, Mass.

The name "Prince" appears but once on Sturbridge, Records between 1722 and 1816, and that once is Juley as above.

V. DAVID (92), son of Stephen and Abigail (Perkins) Prince, was born Jan. 1, 1771, in Sutton, Mass. Married, April 14, 1799, in Oxford, Mass., Rebekah Shumway, who was born Nov. 6, 1780, in Oxford, and was the daughter of Ebenezer Shumway (it is said). She died Aug. 26, 1876, in Oxford, aged 95 years, 9 months, 20 days. He died Sept. 22, 1847, in Oxford, aged 76 years, 8 months, 21 days.

Children.

188. Alpheus, b. Nov. 28, 1799.
189. Rebekah, b. June 3, 1802.
190. Otis, b. Sept. 21, 1805.
191. Almira, b. Mar. 13, 1807.
192. Dave, b. Apr. 6, 1809.
193. David, b. July 22, 1811.
194. Dulsenia, b. Jan. 7, 1814.

195. Zeviah, b. June 9, 1815.
196. Abigail, b. Apr. 14, 1820.
Above children all born in Oxford, Mass.

V. STEPHEN (93), born Nov. 4, 1772, in Sutton, Mass. Died April 18, 1847. Married Abigail Pratt, who was born,   Died of consumption, Oct. 21, 1825, aged 52 years.

Children.

197. Elsie, b. Apr. 28, 1803; m. Oct. 7, 1826, James F. Twiss.
198. Stephen, b. Mar. 15, 1805. He was a merchant in Boston, Mass. Had one child, Mrs. Anna T. Chapman, Ipswich, Mass.
199. Freeman, b. Aug. 2, 1806; m. Nov. 28, 1832, Charlotte Lamb.

V. RACHEL (101), baptized in Thompson, Conn., April 6, 1755. Married there by Rev. Noadiah Russell, April 27, 1780, Phineas Copeland. She died Mar. 9, 1819. They had a daughter, Rachel, who died Nov. 17, 1826. Phineas Copeland was the Executor under the will, of the estate of Joseph Prince. He died Aug. 20, 1813.

V. REBECCA (102), baptized in Thompson, Conn., Feb. 1, 1758. Married there by Rev. Noadiah Russell, Aug.   1790, Elijah Atwood. Died.

V. MARY (103), baptized in Thompson, Conn., April 12, 1763. Married there Nov. 30, 1784, Aaron Bixby,* of Thompson, who was born in 1762, and was son of Nathan Bixby, Jr., and Mary Burrill. He died in Thompson, Dec. 24, 1841, aged 80 years. She also died there, Feb. 22, 1843, aged 79 years, 10 months, 7 days. Dea. Aaron and Mary are both buried in the south-west part of West Thompson cemetery.

---

* Aaron Bixby was a brother of Jemima Bixby, wife of Robert Prince.

Children of Aaron and Mary (Prince) Bixby.

200. Nancy, b. Mar. 5, 1785.
201. Sally, b. Oct. 20, 1788.
202. Joseph, b. Apr. 30, 1791. His wife, Lucy, d. in Thompson, Conn., June 2, 1836, aged 40 years.
203. Aaron, b. Sept. 20, 1800.
204. Mary, b. Nov. 5, 1804; d. Oct. 24, 1862, in Thompson, aged 57 years, 10 months, 19 days.

V. ABEL (106), born in Thompson, Conn.; baptized there Nov. 25, 1759; married there by Rev. Noadiah Russell, Mar. 8, 1782, Lucy Nichols, sister of Squire Jonathan Nichols, of Thompson. After the death of Abel Prince (her husband) she married second, David Brown, and went to live in Brimfield, Mass. She died May 10, 1830, aged 68 years; buried in New Boston, Conn. Think Abel Prince was buried there also, but no headstone to mark his grave. They lived north-west of the present Grosvenordale, on the place since occupied by John Coman.

Children.

205. Lyman, b. in Thompson, Mar. 2, 1793; d. in Douglas, Mass., of lung fever, Mar. 18, 1867, aged 74 years, 16 days.
206. Abel, b. Feb. 18, 1799; d. May 19, 1869, aged 70 years, 3 months, 1 day. He was a stone-cutter by trade. It is said he lived in New London for a time, but died at the Poor House, unmarried. Buried in West Thompson cemetery.
207. George, b.   ; d. in Douglas, Mass., Apr. 11, 1867.
208. Willard, b.   ; d.
209. Lucy, b. about 1784; m. Alpheus Corbin; d.   At one time she was guardian for her four brothers.

On page 436, book 10, of Pomfret Probate Records, is the following:

At a Court of Probate, held at Pomfret, within and for the District of Pomfret, Sept. 6, A. D. 1808,

Present, THOMAS GROSVENOR, ESQ., Judge.

On application of John Prince, guardian to Lyman Prince and Willard Prince; and Alpheus Corbin, guardian to Abel and George Prince, minors of the town of Thompson, to sell the real estate of said minors, lying in said town of Thompson.

Above John Prince (104) was an uncle of Alpheus Corbin's wife, (Lucy Prince.)

V. LUCY (107), born, ; baptized Feb. 12, 1762; married in Thompson, Jan. 27, 1782, by Rev. Noadiah Russell, William Town. He was born Sept. 3, 1758, and was a son of Archelaus and Sarah Town. He died Dec. 25, 1846, aged 88 years, 3 months, 22 days. She died Aug., 1844.

The first four of the following grandchildren are mentioned in the will of Ebenezer Prince.

Children.

210. John, b. ; d.
211. Ebenezer, b. ; d.
212. Rebecca, b. ; d.
213. Dyer, b. ; d.
214. Lucy, b. ; d.
215. Roby, b. ; d.
216. Isaac, b. ; d.

One child died Oct. 5, 1802; another, Oct. 17, 1802; a daughter, Feb. 2, 1823.

[Thompson Church Records.]

V. NATHAN (127), first child of Robert (52) and Jemima (Bixby) Prince, was born Jan. 25, 1777; lived on the

Dodge place, one-half mile north of his father, Robert. Married first, Jerusha, daughter of John Jacobs, who lived north of Brandy Hill, in Thompson. She died Dec. 16, 1819, aged 37 years; buried in Jacobs' burying-ground. Married second, Aug. 5, 1820, by Jonathan Nichols, Mary Carroll, who was born April 28, 1790, and died June 7, 1868, aged 78 years, 1 month, 10 days; buried in West Thompson. She was the fifth of eight children of Nathaniel and Mary Carroll, who were married March 16, 1781. Nathan Prince died April 19, 1859, aged 82 years. Buried in West Thompson cemetery.

See illustration of Nathan Prince's house, built 1816, from timber blown down by the great Sept. gale of 1815. Nathan Prince saw the trees fall one by one, as he sat in the old house which stood about one hundred feet in front of the present house.

Children by First Wife.

217. Sally, b. Feb. 5, 1804; d. Jan. 1, 1887, aged 82 years, 10 months, 26 days; m. Dec. 12, 1825, in Thompson, Theodore Elliott, who d. Aug. 6, 1850, aged 46 years; buried in West Thompson.
218. Julia, b. Mar. 10, 1810; d. Aug. 22, 1842; m. Jan. 1, 1835, by Daniel Dow, Hamilton Ballard, of North Providence, R. I.; buried in East Thompson burying-ground. She was at death aged 32 years, 5 months, 12 days. He d. in Thompson, Feb. 3, 1895, aged 88 years.

Their Children.

Julia Prince Ballard, b.   ; d. when about 2 years old.

Leonidas, b. May 30, 1837, in Providence; now living in Dudley, Mass. P. O. address, Webster, Mass.

219. Mercy, b. Sept. 12, 1816; d. May 25, 1872; buried in Wilsonville, Conn.; m. Jesse Franklin Converse.

NATHAN PRINCE HOUSE.

Children by Second Wife.

220. Jane, b. Sept. 4, 1821; d. Oct. 7, 1878, (single); buried in West Thompson. She spent the last years of her life with her brother Albert, where she died.
221. Albert, b. Sept. 19, 1822; m. Ophelia Elliott.

V. POLLY (131), fifth child of Robert (52) and Jemima Prince, was born in Thompson, Conn., Oct. 22, 1784; died Aug. 31, 1846; married Nov. 3, 1806, John Jacobs, son of Esquire John Jacobs and Dinah (Tourtelotte) Jacobs. He was born in Thompson parish, Killingly, Conn., Sept. 22, 1787; died in Thompson, May 29, 1865, aged 78 years, 8 months, 7 days; buried in West Thompson. He was a farmer and lived in the north part of the town, one-half mile south-east of what is now North Grosvenordale village, on the old turnpike.

Children.

222. Jerusha, b. Nov. 7, 1808; d. Mar. 14, 1836, aged 27 years, 4 months, 7 days, (single); buried in West Thompson yard.
223. Abigail, b Apr. 1, 1810; d. Jan. 17, 1875, aged 64 years, 9 months, 17 days.
224. Delia, b. Jan. 20, 1813; d. Feb. 18, 1878, aged 65 years, 28 days; buried at East Thompson beside her second husband, Harvey Davis.
225. David, b. July 14, 1815; d. Nov. 22, 1835, aged 20 years, 4 months, 8 days, (single); buried in West Thompson.
226. Lorain, b   ; d. (single) July 17, 1866, aged 50 years, 8 months, 22 days.
227. Hannah, b. Oct.   1817; d. Sept. 8, 1821, aged 3 years, 10 months; buried in West Thompson.
228. Mary, b. Feb. 24, 1820; d. Aug. 13, 1882, aged 62 years, 5 months, 19 days.

229. Robert, b. May 4, 1822; d. July 4, 1883, aged 61 years, 2 months.
230. Hannah, b. Mar. 13, 1824; d. Feb. 4, 1888, aged 63 years, 10 months, 21 days; m. Origin Bixby, son of Augustus Bixby. He was b. May 22, 1826; d. Sept. 22, 1879, aged 53 years, 4 days; no issue; buried in West Thompson.

V. ASA (132), sixth child of Robert (52) and Jemima Prince, was born Aug. 21, 1786; died Feb. 21, 1861; married Nov. 24, 1812, by Rev. Daniel Dow, Polly Perrin, who was born in Thompson, west of the present Grosvenordale, and was one of eleven children of "Lieutenant" Daniel and Mary (Dresser) Perrin. She was born July 19, 1786, and died Jan. 24, 1872. They lived at the foot of Dudley Hill, (so called).

Children.

231. Mary, b. May 16, 1814; d.   ; m.
232. David, b. Dec. 26, 1815; d. Dec. 6, 1862, (bachelor).
233. Daniel, b. Sept. 19, 1817; m. Emily Carpenter.
234. John W., b. Aug. 24, 1819; d. Nov. 15, 1883.
235. William, b. June 19, 1822; d. Feb. 8, 1893, aged 70 years, 7 months, 20 days.
236. Louisa, b. Dec. 16, 1824; d. Apr. 9, 1832.
237. Elmira, b. Apr. 5, 1827.
238. Sally Maria, b. Sept. 24, 1829; d. Dec. 1, 1889, (single).
239. George Francis, b. June 1, 1837.

V. ROBERT (135), ninth child of Robert (52) and Jemima Prince, was born Oct. 5, 1795; died Oct. 16, 1866; married in Thompson, Conn., by Rev. Daniel Dow, Hannah Phipps, May 17, 1821. She was born Dec. 28, 1796, and was the sixth of eight children of Jason Phipps. She died Oct. 20, 1853, very suddenly. Robert and Hannah (Phipps) Prince's family lived about one-half mile east of what is now North Grosvenordale, Conn., on the old homestead. See illustration of Robert Prince's house.

DANIEL PRINCE.
PAGE 79. NUMBER 233.

Children.

240. James Monroe, b. Aug. 30, 1822; d. Aug. 17, 1825.
241. Hannah Plimpton, b. Aug. 27, 1824, (single.)
242. Mary Healy, b. Sept. 24, 1826; m. E. Henry.
243. John Adams, b. July 11, 1828; d. Aug. 3, 1891; m. Nancy Maria Marcy.
244. Annie Maria, b. Aug. 27, 1838; m. E. F. Thompson.

V. JEMIMA (136), tenth child of Robert (52) and Jemima Prince, was born April 2, 1797; died Sept. 25, 1856, aged 57 years; married March 27, 1820, by Rev. Daniel Dow, Thomas Benson, Jr., of Thompson. He died Nov. 1, 1869, aged 81 years. They lived and died in Thompson, and were buried in West Thompson cemetery.

Children.

245. Robert Prince, b. May 24, 1821; d.   1863, in New York city.
246. Sarah Key, b. May 1, 1823; m. Oct. 13, 1845, John S. Richardson; P. O. address, (1899), North Grosvenordale, Conn.
247. Alphonso, b. July 28, 1825; m.   1856, Sarah Elizabeth Souls. He d.   and is buried in Worcester, Mass.
248. Mary Ann, b. Jan. 19, 1827; m.   Charles Baker.
249. Jane Davis, b.   1829; d. Sept. 9, 1834.
249A. Cornelia, b. July 11, 1834; d. Apr. 29, 1891; m.   James Humphrey, of Webster, Mass.
250. Thomas, b. Oct. 23, 1835; d. in Thompson, Apr. 21, 1878, aged 42 years, 10 months; m. Apr. 16, 1867, at Worcester, Mass., Sarah Blackstone.
251. Albert, b.   1840, in Thompson; d. Nov. 23, 1863, in Gen'l Hospital, Hilton Head.

V. JOSEPH, JR. (   ),—son of Joseph (54), of Amherst, N. H., who married Dec. 6, 1775, Sarah Wyatt, of Danvers, Mass.,—was born in Amherst, N. H., Oct. 29,

1789; married there Dec. 17, 1812, Hannah Curtis Stiles. (The "Hist. of Amherst" gives the date of their marriage as Mar. 30, 1813; doubtless incorrect, as the first date was furnished by her daughter, Sarah Prince Sucese, of North Vernon, Ind.) She was born at Middleton, Mass., Apr. 1, 1792; died Jan. 13, 1837; was the second child of Cyrus Stiles by his second wife, Hannah Berry. (See "Stiles Genealogy," by Mary Stiles (Paul) Guild, pages 44, 45, 46). [Mrs. Stiles (Paul) Guild's P. O. address, 1898: No. 3 Rindgefield St., North Cambridge, Mass.]

Cyrus Stiles was in the Revolutionary war, in Capt. Nathaniel Lovejoy's Co., Col. Samuel Johnson's Reg't, that marched April 19, 1775, under the command of Lieut. John Adams, to Cambridge, by ye way of Billerica. Cyrus Stiles died at Amherst, N. H., Aug. 24, 1831.

Mr. and Mrs. Prince removed to Warren, Bradford Co., Penn., where she died.

Children.

(Record furnished by Mrs. Sarah A. Prince.)

252. Cynthia Jane, b. July 22, 1814, at Amherst, N. H.; m. Lewis B. Corbin.
253. Nancy Woodbury, b. Oct. 12, 1816; m. Joseph Wright. P. O address, 1895: Owego, Tioga Co., N. Y.
254. Abigail M., b. Feb. 17, 1821.
255. Elmira, b. Jan. 18, 1823; m. Henry Tupper; resided, 1885, at Stevensville, Bradford Co., Penn.
256. George W., b. Feb. 22, 1825; m. Phebe Burbank.
257. Ann Caroline, b. Feb. 22, 1827; m. Francis Bell; P. O. address, 1885: Thompson, Carroll Co., Ill.
258. Joseph Nelson, b. May 21, 1829; P. O. address, 1885, Smithfield, Bradford Co., Penn.
259. Juliet, b. Aug. 8, 1831; d. in infancy.
260. Isadore, b. Mar. 8, 1833; m. Lewis Hines; d. about 1858, in Michigan; left a daughter.

261. Hannah Stiles, b. Apr. 11, 1836; m. T. Bostwick; P. O. address, 1885, Owego, Tioga Co., N. Y. or Penn.
262. Sarah A., b. June 18, 1839; m John M. Sucese, of Montreal, Canada.

V. OLIVER HILLHOUSE (140), youngest child of William (68) and Mary (Hillhouse) Prince, was born 1782, at New London, Conn.; baptized Oct. 7, 1787, by Rev. Rozel Cook, pastor of Montville Cong'l Church; married Aug. 15, 1817. Mary (Ross Norman), eldest daughter of George Norman and Sarah (Grace) Holt, of Lincoln Co., Ga. They settled at Washington, Ga., in 1819; removed to Bibb Co. in 1822, to Milledgeville in 1831, and to Athens, Ga., in 1835. He was State Senator from Bibb Co., and U. S. Senator from Georgia. He was one of the authors of "Georgia Scenes," and compiler of the two digests of Laws of Georgia. He was a man of genuine wit and humor, and a favorite with brethren of the bar. He and his wife were lost Oct. 9, 1837, by the wreck of the steam packet "Home" near Ocracoke Inlet, N. C., where about 100 were drowned.

Children.

263. Mary Raymond, b. Aug. 29, 1819; d. Sept. 15, 1822, in Washington, Ga.
264. George William, b. May 18, 1821; d. Oct. 24, 1822, in Washington, Ga.
265. Oliver Hillhouse, b. Mar. 16, 1823, in Bibb Co., Ga.; m. Sarah, youngest dau. of Henry Jackson, L.L.D.
266. Sarah Virginia, b. Nov. 23, 1825; m. May 5, 1846, Dr. James Mercer Greene.
267. Elizabeth Frances, b. Nov. 7, 1828; m. Apr. 17, 1851, James Roswell King.

V. THOMAS (141), son of Samuel and Mary (Elliott) Prince, was born in Thompson parish, Conn., Oct. 5, 1772; died in Stafford, Conn., Nov. 19, 1842, aged 70 years, 1 month, 14 days; married first, about 1794-5; first wife died in Thompson, Conn., Sept. 1, 1805, as found on record. Married second, Lydia Williams; she died in Stafford, Nov. 13, 1866, aged 76 years. After the death of Thomas, the widow married Abner Holmes, who died July 26, 1864, in Stafford, aged 75 years. No issue.

Children by First Wife.

268. Sanford, b. Sept. 22, 1796; m. Sophia Carr.
269. Sophia, b. Aug. 23, 1798; d. Oct. 14, 1802.
270. Jonathan,* b Aug. 16, 1802; m. Nancy Miller.
271. Huldah, b.   1805; d. Sept. 5,   .

Children by Second Wife.

272. George,* b. Jan. 30, 1809; m. ——— Thompson. Think he d. in New York state, aged about 60 years.
273. Daniel, b.   ; d. July 19, 1837, in Wales, Mass., aged 27 years.
274. Sophia, b. Aug. 12, 1817.
275. Mary Ann, b. Sept. 10, 1818; d.   in Stafford, Conn.; m.   Charles Allen.
276. Huldah, b. Dec. 16, 1822; d.   ; m.   John Stewart, of York, Green Co., Wis.; went to Wisconsin when quite young; d. in Sioux City, Ia.; had child named George Freemont Stewart.
277. Ruby Luvan, b. May 13, 1825; d. Apr. 29, 1892, aged 68 years; m.   Henry Coburn. He d. June 29, 1891, aged 71 years. Both lived and died in Stafford, Conn.

* George and Jonathan when quite young went to Wisconsin.

V. HULDAH (142), born May 19, 1774, in Thompson parish; married there, 1801 (?), to Asa Brackett. He was born   ; died Dec. 26, 1860, in Webster, Mass. She died,

Note: There is on Dudley, Mass., Records an intention of marriage to Asa Brackett, dated Mar. 15, 1801. Probably married about this time. They lived in Dudley and Webster, Mass.

Children.

278. Betsey, b. Mar. 21, 1802.
279. Mary, b. Mar. 27, 1805.
280. Roxiliany, b. Dec. 15, 1807; d. Jan. 9, 1891, in Webster.
281. Huldah, b.   ; d. July 19, 1876, (single,) in Webster, Mass.
282. Prince, b.   ; d. Feb. 8, 1881, in Webster.

The births of the first three, and deaths of the last three, are recorded in Records of Dudley and Webster, respectively.

V. POLLY (143), born Aug. 5, 1775, in Thompson parish, Conn.; died Mar. 8, 1820, in Charlton, Mass., aged 44 years, (g. s.); married Jan. 18, 1798, by Rev. Daniel Dow, Elijah Thompson, of Charlton, Mass. He died Jan. 11, 1842, aged 66 years, (g. s.); buried in Charlton. He married second, May 15, 1821, Clarissa Davis; she died July 3, 1823, aged 37 years, (g. s.).

Children of Polly and Elijah.

283. Thomas Elliott, b. Apr. 29, 1798; d.   ; dancing master 40 years. Probably lived in Barre, Mass.
284. John Dresser, b. Mar. 10, 1800; d.   ; lived in Dudley, Mass. Has son, John, in Providence, R. I., (1895.)

285. Letey, b. Dec. 7, 1801; d.
286. Tyler, b. Jan. 2, 1804; d. Sept. 2, 1865, in Southbridge, Mass.; m.   Abigail Edwards, who was b. Jan. 30, 1808, and d. Aug. 23, 1893.
287. Augusta, b. Apr. 8, 1807; d.   ; m.   Orson Bates; lived and died in Webster; a son, Butler Bates, is in Webster, and has four children.
288. Asenath, b. May 9, 1812.
289. Polly, b. Sept. 8, 1813; d.   in Dudley, Mass.; m.   Leonard Baker.

Above children all born in Charlton, Mass.

(Charlton Records. Kindness of R. B. Dodge, Esq.)

V. DANIEL (144), born in Thompson, Conn., Mar. 18, 1777; died,   ; married   Thankful Tourtellotte, daughter of Capt. Barnabus Tourtellotte, of Thompson, Conn. She died in Thompson, Aug. 8, 1828. It is said that Daniel Prince died there, also.

V. AARON (146), born in Thompson, Conn., Oct. 27, 1779; died in Southbridge, Mass., Jan. 27, 1852, aged 73 years; married in Brooklyn, Conn., Mar. 1, 1802, Sophia Faulkner, of Hampton, Conn. She was born there Apr. 23, 1782. They moved to Southbridge, then to Monson, Mass., then back to Southbridge. She died in Webster, Mass., Mar. 20, 1869, aged 87 years. Both buried in Southbridge.

Children.

290. Mary Maria, b. in Brooklyn, Conn., Nov. 25, 1802; d. in Monson, Mass., Jan.   1894, aged 91 years; m.   John Newton.
291. Caroline, b. May 17, 1804, in Brooklyn, Conn.; d.   in Worcester, Mass.; buried in Southbridge; m.   Silas Gilmore.
292. Louisa, b. in Brooklyn, Mar. 15, 1806; d. in Southbridge, Feb. 1, 1884, aged 78 years; m.   Sullivan Stone.

293. Lucina, b Jan. 23, 1808, in Brooklyn; is now living in Webster, Mass., (1895); m. Josiah Hayes Newton, (a widower), Apr. 4, 1861, in Southbridge, Mass. He was b. ; d. Apr. 15, 1861, in Webster. She now lives on School St., Webster, and is very smart and spry. No issue.
294. Tamson Murdock, b. July 21, 1810, in Brooklyn; d. in Southbridge, May 21, 1822, aged 12 years.
295. Fanny Tucker, b. Mar. 14, 1815, in Dudley, Mass.; is now living in Springfield, Mass, (1895); m. James R. Young.
296. Dell Sophia, b. in Monson, Mass., June 26, 1820; d. in Ware, Mass., Jan. 16, 1847, aged 27 years; buried in Southbridge; m. Merrick Barnes.

V. WILLARD (147), born in Thompson parish, Conn., June 21, 1783; died in East Woodstock, Conn., Apr. 6, 1853, aged 69 years, 8 months, 15 days; buried in Southbridge. Married first, in Thompson, Conn., 1810, Annie Stone. She was born Feb. , 1777; died 1824, aged 46 years; married second, in Thompson, Oct. 8, 1826, by Rev. Daniel Dow, Rhoda Taber. She was born in Tiverton, R. I., 1804; died Aug. 18, 1894, in Webster, Mass., aged 90 years. Buried in Southbridge.

Children by First Wife.

297. Milly N., b. Apr. 27, 1812, in Thompson; m. Addison Pierce.
298. Annie, b. May 1, 1817, in Thompson, Conn.; d. 1848; m. 1836, ———— Willis. Had two boys— Monroe and Jerome.
299. Polly (or Mary), b. 1819; d. 1855; m. Washington Marcy, of Holland, Mass.; had two children—Charles, b. ; lives in Florida. Mary, b.

Children by Second Wife.

300. Rachel V., b. 1827; d. Mar. 12, 1847, aged 20 years.
301. Lucy, b. 1830; d. Feb. 6, 1845, aged 15 years.
302. Harriett N., b. 1832; d. Mar. 4, 1854, aged 22 years.
303. Sarah E., b. 1835; d. Apr. 12, 1859, aged 24 years.
304. Albert Willard, b. 1837; d. July 27, 1857, aged 20 years.
305. Infant, no name, b.   ; d.
306. Lyman Wilson, b. Oct. 1, 1842; living 1899, in Webster, Mass.

(Above children buried in Southbridge, Mass.)

V. ORLAND (149), son of Samuel (71), was born in Thompson, Conn., Nov. 14, 1787; died Dec. 31, 1861, aged 74 years, 1 month, 17 days; lived in Charlton, Mass., and was buried there, (south-west part). Married first, Apr. 4, 1810, Rebecca Gore, who was born Oct. 26, 1791, in Dudley, Mass., and died there Aug. 20, 1836. Married second, Mar. 14, 1837, Adeline Rogers, of Charlton, Mass.

Orland bought the place on which he lived in 1830. Before that time he had lived in Dudley and Southbridge. Married his first wife in Dudley, Mass.

Children by first Wife, Rebecca.

307. Harvey, b. Oct. 3, 1810, in Dudley.
308. Horace, b. Feb. 27, 1812, in Dudley.
309. Orland William, b. Jan. 14, 1814; d. May 1, 1881, in Providence, R. I.; buried there; m. there 1840, Bethania Ailsworth, of that place. No issue.
310. Elliott, b. May 8, 1816, in Dudley; d. Aug. 7, 1886, in Charlton.
311. Harriett, b. in Dudley, May 2, 1818; d. Dec. 26,——; buried in Southbridge, Mass.
312. Lucian, b. Mar. 31, 1820, in Dudley.

313. David, b. Mar. 1, 1822; m. Jennie Belle.
314. Caroline, b. June 7, 1824, in Southbridge.
315. Almira, b. July 29, 1826; m. Horace Edwards.
316. Emeline, b. July 14, 1828, in Southbridge; d. there Oct. 1, 1828.
317. Linus, b. Apr. 24, 1830, in Charlton; d. there Mar. 25, 1831.
318. Infant, unnamed, b. Jan. 2, 1835; d. same day.

Children by Second Wife, Adeline.

319. Sarah Jane, b. Dec. 19, 1837.
320. Linus, b. Feb. 12, 1840.
321. Vernon, b. Dec. 21, 1843; m. Sarah M. Rogers.
322. Charles Henry, b. Jan. 15, 1849.

V. RACHEL (150), was born May 26, 1791; died in Oxford, Mass., June 25, 1822, aged 31 years; married Calvin Phipps. He died Nov. 7, 1822, aged 32 years. They lived, died and were buried in Oxford, Mass. Had two children, who were left orphans; they went to live with, and were brought up by their father's relatives.

Children.

323. George Washington, b. Feb. 22, 1816, in Oxford; m. first, Lucy Ann Littlefield, of Hopkinton, Mass., Apr. 24, 1842. She d. Feb. 2, 1846, aged 24 years. Married second, Jan. 23, 1863, Esther J. Bartlett, of Holliston, Mass. (Both Living, 1895).
324 Mary, b. Dec. 21, 1819; m. Mar. 17, 1870, Dea. Prince Brackett, of Webster, Mass., where he lived. He died Feb. 8, 1881, and was buried there. She (Mary) is now (1899) living with her brother, George W., in Holliston. No issue.

V. AMASA (152), son of Samuel (71), was born in Charlton, Mass., July 14, 1794; died Feb. 18, 1838, in Plainfield, Conn., where he is buried. Married,

Mahala Tourtellotte, daughter of
She was born in Greenfield, N. Y., July 11, 1799; died in Providence, R. I., Mar. 4, 1883.

Children.

325. Lucy, b. in Thompson, Conn., Nov. 25, 1817; m. first, 1842, Arnold Foster, who was b. in Foster, R. I., 1818, and d. in Providence, R. I., June 1854; m. second, 1857, William Wardwell, who was b. in Bristol, R. I., and d. in Providence, 1887. Mrs. Lucy Wardwell's P. O. address is 29 Hoppin street, Providence, R. I.

326. Polly, b. Mar. 20, 1820, in Charlton, Mass.; d. in Roxbury, Mass., Sept. 25, 1894; buried in Providence; m. Nichols Potter, son of Asa Potter, of Sterling, Conn.
    Note: A lame daughter, Anna Potter, works on "Youth's Companion," Boston.

327. Betsey, b. July 15, 1823, in Webster, Mass.; m. John A. Humes, of Pawtucket, R. I. He was b. ; d. in Pawtucket, 1866.
    Betsey Humes' address is 29 Hoppin St., Providence, R. I.

328. Sally, b. July 4, 1826, in Dudley, Mass.; d. Dec. 26, 1827, in Charlton.

329. Samuel, b. Sept. 27, 1828, in Dudley, Mass.; d. 1864, in Providence; buried in Pawtucket. Was married twice; no issue.

330. Sally, b. Aug. 4, 1831, in Webster; d. June 30, 1832, in Webster.

331. Annie, b. May 30, 1833, in Thompson, Conn.; m. ———Martin. P. O. address of Mrs. G. F. Martin: 75 Sabin St., Providence, R. I.

332. Amasa Tourtellotte, b. in Canterbury, Conn., May 20, 1836; d. Oct. 1877, in Chelsea, Mass.,

where he had lived; buried in Pawtucket. He served in the 7th Conn. Reg't. See "Connecticut Soldiers." See "Records of Our Ancestors," by F. A. Prince.

V. JOSEPH (154), second child of (72), was born in Pomfret, Conn., Feb. 17, 1784; died in Brooklyn, Conn., Jan. 9, 1844, aged 60 years, (g. s.); married Jan. 1, 1817, Henrietta Scarborough, (dau. of Samuel). She was born Aug. 21, 1782; died in Westport Point, Mass., Sept. 7, 1874, aged 92 years.

Children.

333. Mary Ann, b. Apr. 4, 1819.
334. Timothy, b. Apr. 18, 1821.

Above children appear on Brooklyn Records.

V. DEIDAMIA (155), was born Jan. 21, 1787; died Feb. 2, 1876, aged 89 years; married Apr. 4, 1811, Philip Scarborough, who was born Feb. 24, 1788, and died in Brooklyn, May 24, 1865. He was the ninth child of Samuel and Mary (Amidon) Scarborough.

Children.

335. Theodore, b. Mar. 19, 1814.
336. Lucy Prince, b. Apr. 16, 1816.
337. Frances A., b. June 22, 1812.
338. Herbert, b. Apr. 6, 1820.

The above is a true copy in the order as they appear on record in the office of Judge of Probate, Brooklyn, Conn.

V. DAVID (156), was born May 22, 1791; died Nov. 21, 1873, in Payson, Ill.; married Apr. 18, 1815, in Brooklyn, Conn., Sophia Ellsworth, who was born Aug. 13, 1794, in East Hartford, Conn. She was the fifth child of Daniel and Mary (Abbot) Ellsworth; died May 3, 1865, in Payson, Ill., of acute pneumonia.

Children.

339. David, b. June 21, 1816; m. first, Mary Jane Dawson.
340. Sophia Ellsworth, b. June 25, 1818; m. Dec. 24, 1840, in Payson, Ill., Samuel M. Helme; d. Oct. 23, 1844, at Payson, of acute pneumonia.
341. Mary Abbot, b. Apr. 17, 1820, in Canadaigua, N. Y.; m. Apr. 26, 1842, in Payson, Ill., Daniel Robbins, who was b. Oct. 15, 1813, in Plymouth, N. H.
342. John Ellsworth, b. Feb. 14, 1825; d. Aug. 23, 1825.
343. Prudence Ann, b. Oct 19, 1826. (Single).
344. Edward, b in West Bloomfield, N. Y., Dec. 8, 1832; graduated from Illinois College in 1852; was lawyer until 1861; cavalry drill master, 1861, and Col. of the 7th Illinois volunteers; civil engineer after the war; member of Am. Society of Civil Engineers. He married in Quincy, Ill., Sept. 24, 1867, Mary Virginia Arthur, who was b. Oct. 18, 1840, in St. Clair Co., Ill., and was dau. of James Arthur and Mary Reed. (Married by Rev. Geo. I. King.)

Children.

Edward, Jr., b. Nov. 1, 1868; d. July 28, 1870.
Edith Ellsworth, b. Apr. 30, 1871.
Mary Abbot, b. Feb. 9, 1880.

Present P. O. address: Quincy, Ill.

For further particulars of war service, see F. A. Prince's "War Records of Our Ancestors."

V. POLLY (157), was born about Nov. 6, 1794; m. Sept. 24, 1827, William Dennison, son of Eleaser Dennison, born,   ; removed to Lancaster, N. H., thence to Buffalo, N. Y., where all the family died many years ago of consumption.

V. BETSEY (159), was born Aug. 16, 1801; died in Buffalo, N. Y.,   ; married,   John M. Denni-

COL. EDWARD PRINCE.
PAGE 64. NUMBER 344.

son, brother of above William. John M. died in Buffalo, N. Y., Jan. 14, 1849, of quinsy.

V. URIAH CADY (162), was born June 17, 1795; died Jan. 3, 1844—drowned himself in a well, in Brooklyn, Conn., where he lived; married Nancy Allen, Sept. 29, 1821.

Children.

345. John Allen, b. Nov. 30, 1822; d. Mar. 25, 1838, aged 15 years.
346. George Frederick, b. Oct. 2, 1827; d. Mar. 5, 1845, aged 17 years; buried in Brooklyn, Conn.

VI. ELZAPHAN (167), born in Danvers, Oct. 22, 1794; married there previous to 1818, Betsey Hiers, who was born Feb. 13, 1799, in Danvers; died July 27, 1835, at Boston.

Children.

347. Elizabeth, b. Apr. 16, 1819.
348. Mary, b. Jan. 16, 1820.
349. Nathan, b. Nov. 9, 1822.
350. Harriet Searle, b. Oct. 16, 1824; d. Aug. 18, 1825.
351. Matthew Hooper, b. Jan. 7, 1835; d. July 26, 1839.

VI. ALPHEUS (188), son of David (92), was born Nov. 28, 1799, in Oxford, Mass.; married there, 1823, Mary Moulton, who was born in Oxford, June 30, 1804, and died in Webster, Mass., July 15, 1876, aged 72 years, 15 days. Alpheus died in Webster, Jan. 17, 1888, aged 88 years, 1 month, 9 days.

Children.

352. Henry, b.   1826; d. in about 6 months; buried in Oxford.
353. James M., b. Dec. 8, 1828, in Oxford. (Children.)
354. Candis M., b.   ; d. Oct. 18, 1861; buried in Webster.

VI. REBEKAH (189), was born in Oxford, Mass., June 3, 1802; died in Oxford, July 28, 1883; buried there; married Feb. 16, 1825, Calvin Hall. He was born in Uxbridge, Mass., Sept. 13, 1791; died in Oxford, Dec. 18, 1870; buried there.

Children.

355. George———, b. Jan. 7, 1826; d. July 17, 1828.
356. Nathan Sumner, b. Aug. 20, 1827; d. Jan. 18, 1882.
357. Luvan Maria, b. Dec. 31, 1828; living (1895) where born.
358. George Calvin, b. Sept. 12, 1830.
359. Austin ———, b. Feb. 26, 1832; d. Aug. 27, 1833.
360. Austin ———, b. May 1, 1835.
361. Jane Judson, b. Oct. 8, 1837; living (1895) where born.

All the above children born in Oxford, Mass.

P. O. address of George Calvin: Buffalo, N. Y.
P. O. address of Austin: Kattellville, Brown Co., N. Y.

VI. OTIS (190), born Sept. 21, 1805; married Mar. 30, 1830, Lois Wadsworth, of Barre, Mass.; at the time of marriage he was of Grafton, Mass. Settled in Barre; was a woolen manufacturer there. He died Apr. 6, 1845. She died,

Children.

362. Henry Warren, b. Oct. 2, 1835.
363. Charles Edwin, b. Aug. 31, 1838; d. July 6, 1839.
364. Adelaide Edwards, b. Apr. 11, 1841; d. Sept. 8, 1841.
365. Fidelia Maria, b. May 19, 1843.

Above children all born in Barre, Mass. From Town Records of Barre.

VI. ALMIRA (191), daughter of David (92), was born Mar. 13, 1807; married first, May 27, 1827, David Hall; he died Apr. 5, 1847; married second, Jeremiah Brown,

June 12, 1858. No issue by Brown. Almira now living, (1895).

Children.

366. Julia E., b. Jan. 17, 1828.
367. Ann Judson, b. Sept. 12, 1832.
368. Judson W., b. Sept. 21, 1838. P. O. address: 17 Chandler St., Worcester, Mass.
369. Ann Jennett, b. May 8, 1845.

VI. DAVID (193), sixth child of David (92), was born in Oxford, Mass., July 22, 1811; married Nov. 14, 1836, Harriett A. Oliver, daughter of James Oliver, of Barre, Mass. Settled in Webster, where he died July 24, 1863; buried in Oxford. His wife died in Worcester, May , 1886; buried in Oxford.

Children.

370. Lewis S., b. Jan. 19, 1838; m. Mrs. Mary Merritt.
371. Sarah Jane, b. May 3, 1842; m. Wm. Walker.
372. Catherine H., b. Oct. 11, 1844; d. Nov. 27, 1864; buried in Oxford.
373. George, b. Aug. 8, 1847; d. young; buried in Oxford.
374. Georgiana, b. Sept. 6, 1849; m. Warren A. Walker.
375. Henry S., b. Nov. 6, 1854; m. Amanda Rand.

VI. DULCENIA C. (194), seventh child of David (92), was born Jan. 12, 1814; married first, Sept. 10, 1834, George M. Eames. He was born 1811, in Framingham, Mass; died   1851, aged 41 years; buried in Framingham. She married second,   1858, L. W. Merrifield, of West Boylston, Mass. He died about 1870-5. She died 1891, aged 78 years; buried in Worcester, Mass.

Children by First Husband.

376 Mary Ann, b.   1836; d.   1858, aged 22 years; m. B. F. Hatch, of Worcester. He d. about 1885; both buried in Worcester. No issue.

377. George P., b. Dec. 1, 1838; m. first, 1857, Sarah M. Cole, of Londonderry, N. H.; (now living); m. second, 1865, Laura A. Hale, of New York city. She was b. Dec. 30, 1848; d.   1893, in Worcester, Mass., aged 45 years. George Eames now living; had four children, all dying in infancy; buried in Worcester. George Eames' P. O. address: No. 9 Bellevue St., Worcester, Mass.

VI. ZEVIAH (195), eighth child of David (92), was born June 9, 1815; married July 14, 1842, Arnold Anthony, of Worcester, Mass. She died Dec. 13, 1882. He died Dec. 17, 1871.

Children.

378. Sarah Jane, b. June 27, 1843; m. May 16, 1866, M. A. Maynard, of Worcester. P. O. address: Box 609 Worcester, Mass.
379. Julia Ann, b. Mar. 11, 1845.
380. Sophia ——, b. Mar. 1, 1848; d. Sept. 6, 1849.
381. Charles Francis, b. June 6, 1850.
382. Henry Augustus, b. Jan. 1, 1854.
383. George Edwin, b. Dec. 20, 1856.
384. Sophia Elizabeth, b. Sept. 6, 1858; m. May 4, 1876, Charles B. Richardson.

VI. ABIGAIL (196), ninth child of David (92), was born Apr. 14, 1820; married first, Apr. 7, 1840, Elbridge Corbin, of Webster, Mass.; one child. Married second, Orris Parsons, of Worcester, Mass.; three children. She died Oct.   1880, at Westboro, Mass.

VI. ELSIE (197), born Apr. 28, 1803; m. Oct. 7, 1826, James F. Twiss.

Children.

385. Stephen, b   ; m.   . Lawyer in Kansas City, Mo., and has been Mayor.

386. Amos, b.   ; m.   ; lives in Worcester.
387. Abbie, b.   ; m. Mr.——— Brewer; lives in Ashton, Lee Co., Ill.

VI. FREEMAN (199), born Aug. 2, 1806; married Nov. 28, 1832, Charlotte Lamb, of Charlton, Mass. She was born Sept. 13, 1811; died July 5, 1880, in Worcester, Mass., of peritonitis. He died Aug. 23, 1852, in Oxford, Mass., of quick consumption. He was a farmer at Oxford.

Children.

388. Abigail, b. Oct. 8, 1833, in Oxford; d. Dec. 28, 1835, of scarlet fever.
389. Sarah, b. June 30, 1835, in Oxford; d. June 17, 1858, of consumption.
390. Samuel, b. Aug. 30, 1837, in Oxford; d. July 7, 1848, of convulsions.
391. Albert, b. July 4, 1839, in Oxford; was Capt. in 15th Mass. Reg't. See F. A. Prince's "War Records." Married Dec. 23, 1869, Miss S. J. Dyke. He died Mar. 2, 1881, of paralysis, in Worcester.
392. Emily, b. Oct. 23, 1841, in Oxford; m. Alexander Searles, Oct. 2, 1877.
393. Mary, b. Jan. 20, 1844; m. Peleg Freeman Murray; resides in Worcester; one child,—Chas. Bernard, b. Apr. 6, 1866.
394. Edward, b. Nov. 30, 1846, in Oxford; m. Jan. 18, 1871, Katy D——— Robinson. She d. July 25, 1872. He m. second, May 22, 1878, Mrs. H. E. Lee. Had one child by first wife,—Harry, b. Apr. 12, 1872; d. July 13, 1872. Mrs. H. E. Prince's present P. O. address is, 3 Conduit St., Prov., R. I. His whereabouts unknown; he left her in Dec., 1885, and not heard from since.
395. Ann Maria, b. Feb. 11, 1850, in Oxford; m. Charles S. Day, Oct. 20, 1871, Worcester, Mass. One child,—Alice May, b. Sept. 13, 1872.

VI. LYMAN (205), son of Abel (106), was born in Thompson, Conn., Mar. 2, 1793; died in Douglas, Mass., of lung fever, Mar. 18, 1867, aged 74 years, 16 days. He was a cooper by trade; lived on old homestead about one and a half miles north-west of Grosvenordale, Conn.; place since occupied by John Coman. He married   , Polly Corbin, sister of Alpheus Corbin.

Children.

396. Emily, b. Jan. 2, 1811; m.   , Anson Barrett.
397. Mary Ann, b June 6, 1819; m.   , Alpheus Albee; settled in Charlton, Mass. P. O. address: Southbridge, Mass.
398. Loren, b. about Mar. 7, 1821.
399. Eunice, b.   ; d. Sept. 20, 1832, aged 4 years; buried at New Boston, Conn.

Above children born in Thompson. Loren is on Thompson Poor Farm, (1897).

VI. GEORGE (207), son of Abel (106), was born in Thompson, Conn.,   ; died in Douglas, Mass., Apr. 11, 1867; married   , Georgiana ———, born   ; died   . He was a carpenter by trade; lived, and worked for a time, at the present Grosvenordale, Conn.

Children.

400. Jerome, b.
401. Georgiana, b.   ; d.   when a young woman.

VI. LUCY (209), daughter of Abel (106), was born in Thompson, Conn., about 1784; died June 22, 1849, aged 65 years; married in Thompson, by Rev. Daniel Dow, Alpheus Corbin (a brother of Polly Corbin), Feb. 5, 1805, as recorded in old family Bible. Church records has it as married June 3, 1805. He used to operate grist-mill at the present Grosvenordale, Conn.; also colored homespun yarn for families in that vicinity. Lived at or near the place long since occupied by John Coman, north-west of the above place. "Captain" Alpheus Corbin, as he was called, died Jan. 28, 1853, in Thompson

The following record, furnished by their granddaughter, Mrs. Ellen D. Adams, (dau. of Caroline, No. 402) of North Oxford, Mass., was found in their old family Bible, in Ohio, Dec., 1896.

Children.

402. Caroline, b. May 8, 1806; d. June   , 1894; m. Porter Edwards.
403. Harriett, b Aug. 21, 1808; m   , George Dillaber. Had child, George. It is said they lived and died at or near the Haskell place, so called, at Pomfret, Conn.
404. John Prince, b. Jan. 13, 1812; d. Apr. 20, 1812, aged 3 months, 7 days
405. John Prince, b. Aug. 3, 1813; d. Feb. 5, 1815, aged 1 year, 6 months, 2 days.
406. Lucy Nichols, b. Nov. 28, 1818; m.   , ——— Chase; living in Ohio, 1896.
407. Emeline, b. Mar. 7, 1820; d.   , in Philadelphia, Pa.
408. George Alpheus, b. Apr. 28, 1822; d. Aug. 30, 1824, aged 2 years, 4 months, 4 days; buried in West Thompson.
409. Eunice Ann, b. Sept. 3, 1825; d. in Reading, Pa.

VI. SALLY (217), first child of Nathan (127), was born Feb. 5, 1804; died Jan. 1, 1887, aged 82 years, 10 months, 26 days; married in Thompson, Conn., Dec. 12, 1825, Theodore Elliott. who was born   ; d. Aug. 6, 1850, aged 46 years; buried in West Thompson cemetery.

Children.

410. Mary (who was called Polly), b. in Thompson, Conn., Dec. 29, 1827; m. Mar. 1, 1847, by Rev. Daniel Dow, Horace Elliott, son of Thomas Elliott, Jr.,

and Polly (Dexter) Elliott. She d. July 5, 1886; buried in West Thompson. They lived in Thompson. Had one child,—Emergene, b. June 8, 1849; m.   ,   Williams.

411. Oscaforia J———, b. in Thompson, Conn., Aug. 31, 1844; m. June 28, 1870, in Webster, Mass., by Rev. J. V. Osterhout, Rev. Lyman Partridge, (Baptist minister). They now live (1897) at West Dedham, Mass. Their children are as follows:—

Herbert Graves, b. Oct. 20, 1871. Herbert G. Partridge was appointed assistant physician of the Rhode Island Hospital in Providence, R. I., and commenced his duties in the autumn of 1895. He graduated from Brown University in 1892, and in June, 1895, from the Medical School of the University of Pennsylvania.

Theodore Elliott, b. Apr. 21, 1873; d. Oct. 24, 1874, aged 18 months.

VI. MERCY (219), third child of Nathan (127), by first wife, Jerusha (Jacobs) Prince, was born in Thompson, Conn., Sept. 12, 1816; died May 25, 1872, aged 55 years, 8 months; buried in Wilsonville, Conn.; married by Rev. H. Fitts, pastor of Thompson Baptist church, May 21, 1837, Jesse Franklin Converse, who was born in Pomfret, Conn., Apr. 20, 1815; now living in Thompson, (1899). He enlisted in the Civil war, Aug. 4, 1862, serving in the 18th Conn. Vols.; mustered in Aug. 18, 1862; mustered out with honorable discharge, disability, July 29, 1864. His son, Joel T., enlisted and mustered in Jan. 4, 1864; wounded and captured at Piedmont, Va., June 5, 1864; died Aug. 30, 1864, in Andersonville prison, Ga. He served in Co. D, 18th Conn. Vols.

Children.

412. George Franklin, b. Feb. 27, 1839; d. Feb. 13, 1843.
413. Joseph T——, b. Aug. 5, 1842; d. July 26, 1846.
414. George, b. Apr. 5, 1844; d. May 23, 1844.
415. Joel T——, b. June 15, 1846; d. Aug. 30, 1864; m. just previous to enlisting, Betsey Shumway, of Webster, daughter of John Shumway.
416. Mary E., b. July 1, 1854; m. in Wilsonville, Conn., by Rev. James S. Thomas, Thursday evening, Nov. 28, 1872, H—— Davis Bates, son of Ira Bates, of Thompson. They have had seven children; four living. Present address: 1028 Hancock St., Brooklyn, N. Y.

VI. ALBERT (221), second child of Nathan (127), by second wife, was born in Thompson, Conn., Sept. 19, 1822; married there May 12, 1844, by Rev. Charles Curtis Barnes, (first Methodist minister at the present North Grosvenordale, Conn.) Ophelia Elliott, who was born in Thompson, Oct. 18, 1825, and was the first child of Dyer Nichols and Eliza (Green) Elliott, of Thompson. Dyer N. Elliott died Mar. 20, 1893, aged 95 years, 3 months, 12 days. Eliza (Green) Elliott died Mar. 3, 1885, aged 83 years, 10 days. Albert Prince was born and lived about one-half mile north of the Robert Prince homestead. (See illustration). He and his father, Nathan, carried on the farm until 1858, when he saw what he considered a better opening for farming, and bought one of the best farms in East Woodstock, Conn., which is located on very high ground overlooking the country for miles around. Beautiful scenery surrounds them on all sides, and no less than seven church spires can be counted. Mr. Prince possessed no political aspirations, neither aspired to office of any kind, but devoted his attention to the duties which pertain to farming.

Children.

417. Mary Ophelia, b. in Thompson, Oct. 9, 1845; m. Allen Barber Richmond.

418. Francis Albert, b. in Thompson, May 15, 1851;
   m. Sarah Maria Chaffee.
419. Jerusha Jacobs, b. in Thompson, May 12, 1856;
   m. Edward Francois Richardson.
420. Louis Elliott, b. in East Woodstock, Mar. 31, 1862;
   d. there Apr. 4, 1879, of pneumonia. Buried in West Thompson cemetery.

Albert and Ophelia (Elliott) Prince, on May 12, 1894, celebrated their golden wedding anniversary, and the following poem was written for the occasion by their grandson, Charles Henry Prince.

A FIFTY SUMMER VOYAGE.

I'm not much of a poet,—
  Rhymer, I like much better;
So you need not call this a poem,
  Just call it a family letter.

We have assembled here,
  A little band, absorbed in country lore,
With congratulations and old time yarns
  Since the days of forty-four.

From different sources we've come,
  As in the good old days of yore,
There's always a fire on the hearthstone,
  A warm greeting at the door.

The circle about you is almost complete,
  Here are fathers and mothers and brothers,
All wishing the same long life and health,
  Misters and sisters and others.

We all join in with one accord,
  In the quaint old-fashioned way,
Both young and old, the timid, the bold,
  Upon this festive day.

This is our cry, it's loud, it's long,
   As it falls upon our senses,
"Long live the king," "Long live the queen,"
   And long, long live the Princes.

But hark! catch the echo as it clearly sounds
   In response to this our cry;
Though man may fall and pass away,
   His works shall never die.

And if we're not the same dear friends
   You in your youth did know,
We love you as they did who met
   Just fifty years ago.

This is your golden wedding day,
   The diamond is to follow,
The others all were yesterday,
   And this is but to-morrow.

There's many a change since you came home
   As bridegroom and as bride;
Your little ones have all grown up,
   Been borne out with the tide,

But there's one chair that's vacant,
   And the picture on the wall
Reminds us of him who has left you,
   Answering to the heavenly call.

He was the first to leave you,
   But follow all, we must;
It is sad, but bright the outlook
   With an unfaltering trust.

Since forty-four, those days of yore,
   By storm and sunshine tried,
In changing wind and weather
   Have you roughed it side by side.

Wise sailors you have both become
　　Upon this voyage of life,
For the captain is a noble man,
　　The pilot a noble wife.

The voyage is fifty summers long,
　　The race is almost run,
And 'tis little I know of its calms and storms,
　　Son of your son.

To me it is now tradition,
　　You've landmarks that are gray,
And you alone can tell the happenings
　　Of years ago to-day.

But I've garnered from your stories
　　Of pleasure and of care,
Many thoughts of dear remembrance,
　　Clinging close to grandpa's chair.

For this is *home*, how dear the name,
　　How quiet like and still,
We love it all the more because
　　It's way up on the hill.

And you have lived up here alone
　　And carried on the farm,
Through stormy seas, till close to port,
　　You're sailing in a calm.

The flickering lights gleam faintly,
　　As the life boat nears the shore,
Faith and hope keep it from sinking,
　　And will keep it evermore.

Pause a little ere the landing,
　　Just one look back o'er the sea,
One reflection, then 'tis finished,
　　What I have to offer thee.

ALBERT PRINCE.
PAGE 73. NUMBER 221.

OPHELIA (ELLIOTT) PRINCE.
PAGE 73.

Your lives are as the wheat field,
  That is heavy with golden grain,
For ye've lived unto God's glory,
  Ye have not lived in vain.

Will others say the same of us
  Who live in years to come?
God grant us all a golden voyage,
  And a golden harvest home.

VI. ABIGAIL [223], second child of Polly Prince (131), and John Jacobs, was born in Thompson, Conn., Apr. 1, 1810; died Jan. 17, 1875; married Nov. 29, 1838, by Rev. Daniel Dow, Marquis Jacobs, son of Ezra Jacobs, of Thompson, being her own cousin. He died Sept. 1, 1869, aged 57 years, 5 months, 5 days.

They had one child:—

421. Ann Maria, b. May 11, 1841; d. June 23, 1842, aged 13 months, 12 days.

VI. DELIA (224), third child of Polly Prince (131), and John Jacobs, was born Jan. 20, 1813; died Feb. 18, 1878; married first, , Benjamin Carleton, a widower, and farmer of East Thompson. He died July 26, 1866, aged 54 years, 3 months, 18 days. She married second, Sept. 9, 1868, by Rev. W. A. Worthington, pastor of Brandy Hill church, Harvey Davis, a widower, and farmer of East Thompson. He died Feb. 23, 1890, aged 81 years, 3 months, 26 days. They are both buried by the side of each other in East Thompson. No issue by either husband.

VI. MARY (228), seventh child of Polly Prince (131,) and John Jacobs, was born Feb. 24, 1820; died Aug. 13, 1882, aged 62 years, 5 months, 19 days; married in Thompson, by Rev. Daniel Dow, Dec. 8, 1839, Sylvester Elliott. He died Aug. 17, 1871, aged 54 years, 5 months. Both buried in West Thompson.

VI. ROBERT (229), son of Polly Prince (131), and John Jacobs, was born May 4, 1822; died July 4, 1883, aged 61 years, 2 months; married Dec. 16, 1846, Sally Elliott, daughter of Thomas Elliott, Jr., and sister of Horace Elliott. She died June 20, 1886, aged 61 years, 9 months, 18 days.

Children.

422. John Elliott, b. Feb. 3, 1848; m. Sept. 23, 1873, Nettie Baker, of N. Y.
423. Mary Elizabeth, b. June (or Jan.) 16, 1850; d. Sept. 23, 1873. (?)
424. Henry Dexter, b. Dec. 19, 1852; m. first, Etta Wallace; m. second, Isabel Hamm, of Chelsea.
425. Addie J——, b. Sept. 7, 1855.
426. Emma Augusta, b. May 22, 1858; m. Sept. 26, 1883, Dr. C. S. Sargent, of Webster, Mass.

VI. MARY (231), first child of Asa (132), was born May 16, 1814; married June 2, 1832, Charles Barnes Elwell. He was born Nov. 18, 1808; died June 7, 1878; lived, died and was buried in Dudley, Mass.

Children.

427. Jane Louisa, b. Mar. 26, 1833.
428. William Clifford, b. Mar. 27, 1839; d. Sept. 23, 1840.
429. George Francis, b. July 31, 1841; d. July 14, 1864.
430. Emily Frances, b. Feb. 7, 1844; d. Dec. 2, 1875; m. Oct. 6, 1866, Erastus B—— Durkee.
431. Elizabeth, b. Apr. 5, 1847.
432. Mark, b. Sept. 2, 1849.
433. Callie Maria, b. July 7, 1851; d. Dec. 13, 1883; m. May 3, 1873, John W—— Young.
434. Sallie Barnes, b. Oct. 21, 1856; m.   , George A—— Burnett.

VI. DANIEL (233), third child of Asa (132), was born Sept. 19, 1817; now living with his only child, Emily M., in Quincy, Ill.; married Sept. 8, 1842, at Charlton, Mass., by Rev. —— Haven, (Cong'l minister), Emily Carpenter, who was the third child of Leonard and Matilda (Reynolds) Carpenter, and was born   , in Charlton, Mass., and died   , in Dudley, Mass. Daniel, several years ago, was a farmer and lived about one mile northwest of Dudley Academy, on the road from Dudley to Southbridge, Mass.

Child.

435. Emily Marilla, b. in Dudley, Mass., Aug. 31, 1844.

VI. JOHN WHITNEY (234), fourth child of Asa (132), was born Aug. 24, 1819; died Nov. 15, 1883, in Dudley, Mass., and was buried there. He lived on his father's old homestead in Dudley. Married June 7, 1866, Lucretia J. Alby, of Milford, Mass. She is now living in Southbridge, Mass., 1899.

Children.

436. John Dudley, b. July 1, 1870; m. in Thompson, May 3, 1892, Lillian Barnes of New Boston, Conn.
437. Ethel Louise, b. July 20, 1874; m. by Rev. G. W. Penniman, of Southbridge, Sept. 19, 1897, James H. Babcock, of New York City. After marriage they spent the winter in Central America, returning in the spring to New York. Mr. Babcock is manager of a hotel in New York, having begun in the business as a bellboy. Miss Prince was a clerk in the postoffice at Southbridge for some time.

VI. WILLIAM (235), fifth child of Asa (132), was born in Dudley, Mass., June 19, 1822; died Feb. 8, 1893, aged 70 years, 7 months, 19 days; m.   , 1855, Catherine Harwood, of Oxford, Mass. She died Oct. 10, 1895;

buried at New Boston, Conn. William was a farmer and lived near to, and in sight of his father's. Farms joined.

Children.

438. Alice Maria, b. Feb. 6, 1859.
439. Fannie Lucetta, b. Nov. 22, 1860; d. Mar. 12, 1880.
440. Mary Ella, b. June 5, 1862; m. Mar. 23, 1892, William Bradbury Chandler, sixth and last child of William and Abigail Chandler, of Thompson. Present P. O. address of W. B. Chandler is, North Grosvenordale, Conn.
441. Willie Asa, b. Feb. 6, 1868; m. Apr. 8, 1896, Jennie Desrosiers, of Worcester, Mass.; have two children:—Ernest William, b. Jan. 4, 1897; Harry Leon, b. Feb. 17, 1898.

VI. ELMIRA (237), seventh child of Asa (132), was born Apr. 5, 1827; married Apr. 6, 1852, by Rev. Phineas Heesy, of Dudley, Lucian Milton Barnes, who was born Nov. 18, 1828, and died in Dudley, Mass., Dec. 28, 1873; buried at New Boston, Conn.

Children.

442. Halsey H——, b. Jan. 26, 1853; d. Jan. 16, 1877.
443. Hattie Frances, b. Nov. 21, 1855; d. Aug. 6, 1856.
444. Hattie Frances, b. Jan. 22, 1857; m. Oct. 5, 1882, James Edward Larned, who was b. ——, and was the ——— child of——.
445. Herbert Wesley, b. Apr. 11, 1858; m. Oct. 18, 1883, Mary E—— Lowe, who was b.——.
446. Ada Louise, b. July 22, 1860; d. Mar. 24, 1864.
447. Davis Mason, b. Apr. 5, 1863; d. Mar. 25, 1864.
448. Edwin Milton, b. May, 29, 1865.
449. James Lincoln, b. Mar. 15, 1867.

WILLIAM PRINCE.
PAGE 79. NUMBER 235.

VI. MARY HEALY (242), third of five children of Robert (135), and Hannah (Phipps) Prince, was born in Thompson, Conn., Sept. 24, 1826; married Aug. 11, 1853, in Thompson, at home, by Rev. E. F. Hinks, Erastus Henry, who was born in Rochester, N. Y., in 1818, and was the first of five children of Erastus and Elizabeth (Putnam) Henry, of Rochester. He died in Worcester, Mass., without issue, Aug. 2, 1883, aged 65 years, and was buried there in Hope cemetery, on Forest Ave. Soon after marriage they moved to Savannah, Ga., meeting with much prosperity. They lived there through the war, and until 1879, when they returned to Worcester, Mass. After his death the widow (Mary) returned to the old homestead where she now lives, 1899, with her sister Annie.

VI. JOHN ADAMS (243), fourth of five children of Robert (135), and Hannah (Phipps) Prince, was born in Thompson, Conn., July 11, 1828; married first, June 4, 1855, at the parsonage of Rev. Warren Emerson, North Grosvenordale, Conn., Nancy Maria Marcy, who was the first of four children of Gurdon and Fidelia Marcy, of West Woodstock, Conn. She was born   ; died Feb. 10, 1863, aged 27 years. He married second, Jan. 1, 1867, in Worcester, Mass., by the Rev. Dr. Hill, Charlotte Townsend, (maiden name) widow of George Buxton, of Marlboro, N. H. She was born   ; now lives at "Prospect pect Farm," in Leicester, Mass., (1899). John died Aug. 3, 1891, aged 63 years, 23 days; buried in Hope cemetery, Forest Ave., Worcester, Mass.

Child by First Wife.

450. Robert Henry, b. May 19, 1861; d. Feb. 10, 1865.

Children by Second Wife.

451. Bertha May, b. in Worcester, Sept. 7, 1869; m. J. G. Schmohl.

452. Nora Hannah, b. in Worcester, May 6, 1875; m. Sept. 12, 1894, Alexander Nichols Smith, who was born——. Now live in Fitchburg, Mass., (1899).

VI. ANNIE MARIA (244), fifth child of Robert (135), and Hannah (Phipps) Prince, was born in Thompson, Conn., Aug. 27, 1838; married Jan. 31, 1870, at home, in Thompson, by Rev. S. H. Fellows, Edward Freeman Thompson, who was born June 11, 1839, and was the first of nine children of Hiram and Betsey (Studley) Thompson, of Slatersville, R. I. They live on the original Prince homestead, (1899). Without issue. (See illustration of Robert Prince's house.) The original house of Robert Prince was on the west side of the road; the present one is on the east side, just opposite of where the old one stood. Mr. Thompson is a wide-awake, popular and prosperous farmer; prominent in local affairs, and has served on School Board and various town offices; has filled all positions of trust and responsibility in a faithful and judicious manner. On Nov. 8, 1898, he was elected to represent the town in the Legislature by an overwhelming majority. Both Mr. and Mrs. Thompson have gained for themselves the honors they so richly deserve. They are earnest and efficient workers in church affairs, always faithfully serving with great liberality.

Hannah Plimpton and Mary Healy enjoy the hospitable home of their sister, Mrs. Thompson, the home of their birth.

VI. SARAH A. (262), daughter of Joseph, Jr., was born June 18, 1839; married John M. Sucese, of Montreal, Canada, June 2, 1842. Mr. Sucese took a course in the Homeopathic Medical College, Philadelphia, Penn., and graduated from the Eclectic Medical College at Cincinnati, Ohio. He died——. In 1885 his wife was living at North Vernon, Jennings Co., Ind.

Children.

453. John Prince, b. Mar. , 1843; m. , Julia Sellard. He served in the Union army during the War of the Rebellion. P. O. address, 1885: Troy, Bradford Co., Penn.
454. Joseph Hahnemann, b. Sept. 21, 1848; was a Union soldier during the Civil war; d. Jan. 26, 1874, from disease contracted in the service.
455. Jay B., b. June 13, 1850; m. , 1885, Ada Durham; was a railroad conductor, and resided at North Vernon, Ind.
456. Josie M., b. Nov. 25, 1854; m. , A. J. Johnson, a railroad conductor; resided, 1885, at North Vernon, Ind.
457. Jasmine, b. Apr. 18, 1857; graduated from a College in Danville, Ind., July 20, 1880; is a school teacher by profession.
458. Jennie, b. Jan. 10, 1859; graduated with highest honors from the public schools of North Vernon; afterwards taught music and was also an instructor in the schools; m. , John R. Tague, a druggist; resided at Memphis, Tenn.

VI. OLIVER HILLHOUSE (265), third child of Oliver H. Prince (140), was born Mar. 16, 1823, in Bibb Co., Ga.; married June 15, 1852, Sarah Maria, youngest daughter of Henry Jackson, L. L. D., and Martha, his wife. He studied law and was admitted to the bar, but never practiced. Before his marriage he was, for some years, editor of the "Macon Telegraph," and was a writer of some note. His "Billy Woodpile" letters were written during the exciting period just before the Civil war, and were full of clever personalities and political hits. After his marriage he was a planter in upper and south-western Georgia. He died in Decatur, Ga., Jan. 22, 1875. His wife, Sarah Maria (Jackson) Prince, was born June 9, 1824, and is still living, (1896).

Children.

459. Martha Basiline Hillhouse, b. July 19, 1855. Address: No. 9, Halifax Square, Brunswick, Ga.
460. Oliver Hillhouse, b. Nov. 19, 1857, in   ; d. Apr. 30, 1885, of pulmonary tuberculosis; was a clerk in the Treasury Dept., at Washington, under the Civil Service law, at the time of his death.
461. Henry Rootes Jackson, b. Nov. 15, 1859, in   ; is a railroad clerk in Louisville, Ky.; m. Apr.   , 1884, Marie Jane, eldest dau. of John and Mary Turley. She was b.——.
462. Marie Jacqueline, b. Nov. 10, 1861; m. Apr. 29, 1884, Jordan Sumner Thomas.

VI. SARAH VIRGINIA (266), fourth child of Oliver H. Prince (140), was born Nov. 23, 1825, in Bibb Co., Ga.; married May 5, 1846, Dr. James Mercer Greene, second son of William Montgomery Greene and Jane McConkey. He was a physician and lived in Macon, where he died   , 1881, of——.

William Montgomery Greene was born and educated in Ireland, and escaped thence in 1800, having been engaged in the revolution attempted by Lord Edward Fitz-Gerald. He was educated at Trinity College, Dublin; was a Prof. in University at Athens, Ga. He died in Macon, Ga., June   , 1846. Jane (McConkey) Greene died in Milledgeville, Ga , about 1827.

Children.

463. Mary Raymond, b. Jan. 16, 1847; d. Aug. 26, 1877.
464. Henry McConkey, b. July 28, 1848; d. Aug. 21, 1874.
465. Oliver Hillhouse, b. Dec. 31, 1849; d. Mar. 10, 1877; m. Dec. 23, 1873, Cornelia Hanson.

466. William Montgomery, b. Aug. 19, 1851; d. Mar. 15, 1853.
467. Francis Mitchell, b. May 17, 1853; d. Oct. 2, 1853.
468. Virginia Selina, b. July 9, 1855; m. Feb. 21, 1882, William Ashe Poe.
469. James Edward Beauregard, b. Aug. 21, 1861; single; is a physician, and lives at 557 McDonough St., Brooklyn, N. Y.

VI. ELIZABETH FRANCES (267), fifth child of Oliver H. Prince (140), was born Nov. 7, 1828; died Jan. 5, 1880; married Apr. 17, 1851, James Roswell King, a manufacturer, of Roswell, Ga., and third son of Barrington and Mary Nephew King, of the above place. James Roswell King married second,——.

Children.

470. Harriet Buell, b. Mar. 6, 1852; d. young.
471. Barrington James, b. Apr. 29, 1854.
472. Oliver Hillhouse, b. Mar. 1, 1856.
473. Charles, b. Oct. 4, 1857.

It is said there were ten children.

VI. SANFORD (268), first child of Thomas (141), by first wife, was born in Thompson, Conn., Sept. 22, 1796; died at Mongaup Centre, Sullivan Co., N. Y.,   , 1879; married   , 1818, Sophia Carr, in town of Ashford, Windham Co., Conn.

John M. Prince says that Sanford was born in Berkshire Co., Mass. The Records have it same as above,—Thompson.

Children.

474. William S., b. Sept. 20, 1820.
475. Orrin, b. Apr. 19, 1822.

476. John M., b. June 20, 1824.
477. Laura S., b. May 9, 1828.
478. Elmira J., b. Aug. 15, 1831.
479. Caroline, b. Aug. 10, 1836.
480. James F., b. Dec. 5, 1839.
481. Mary E., b.   , 1842.

VI. JONATHAN (270), third child of Thomas (141), was born in Thompson, Conn., Aug. 16, 1802; died at Osage, Mitchell Co., Iowa, Apr. 14, 1876; married first, May 14, 1824, in West York, Nancy Miller. She died Sept. 15, 1854, of cholera, in Primrose, Dane Co., Wis; buried in Wm. Green cemetery, town of York, Green Co., Wis. He married second, Mrs. Emeline M. Vanderbilt, (widow). She had two children, Ellen and Louisa. She died previous to his death,——. Jonathan, soon after marriage, lived and worked in Black Rock, N. Y., as a molder, about two years and a half; then moved to Lady, N. Y., where he worked in foundry and machine shop for about fourteen years. Moved from there to Otto, Cattaraugus Co., N. Y., where he lived for several years; went from there to Coltspring, Penn., in 1844; went from there in July, 1845, to Wisconsin territory, landing in town of York, Green Co., Aug. 17, 1845; took up a claim of 160 acres in town of Primrose, Dane Co. When Wisconsin was made a state he was elected a Justice of the Peace. Afterwards sold his farm and moved, in 1859, to Cameran, Mo. At the breaking out of the Rebellion, rebels took about all he had, and he returned back to Mitchell Co., Iowa, where he owned a quarry and lime kiln, and died at Osage, Iowa.

Children by First Wife.

482. Sophia, b. Jan. 29, 1826, in Buffalo, N. Y.; d. June 11, 1894.
483. Lucy M., b. Jan. 1, 1830, in Lady, N. Y.; living at Lynxville, Wis., 1896.

484. Alva T., b. Mar. 29, 1832, in Lady, N. Y.; d. Jan.   , 1836.
485. Sanford C., b. May 17, 1838, in Otto, N. Y.
486. Nancy Ledicia, b. July 26, 1840, in Otto, N. Y.; living at Lynxville, Wis., 1896.
487. Mary Luvan, b. Mar. 2, 1844, in Coltspring, Penn.; is at present (1896) insane, caused by breaking a needle in her hand. Surgeons could not get it out; been so for about ten years; is at asylum in Grant Co., Wis.

VI. SOPHIA (274), daughter of Thomas (141), by second wife, was born in Monson, Mass., or Stafford, Conn., Aug. 12, 1817; died Nov. 30, 1892; married Nov. 9, 1836, John Sherman, by Festus Foster, of Brimfield, Mass.

Children.

488. Lewis, b.   ; P. O. address: 15 Washington St., Worcester, Mass.
489. John A., b.   ; P. O. address: 24 Deane St., Worcester, Mass.
490. George, b.   ; P. O. address: Winthrop St., Taunton, Mass.
491. Roger, b.   ; P. O. address: 85 South St., Concord, N. H.

Above children all born in Brimfield, Mass.

VI. MARY MARIA (290), first child of Aaron (146), and Sophia, his wife, was born Nov. 25, 1802, in Brooklyn, Conn.; married Sept.   , 1825, John Newton, of Monson, Mass., with whom she became acquainted while living there with her parents. He died Dec.   , 1871. She died in Monson, Jan.   , 1894, aged 91 years.

Children.

492. Charles O., b   ; address (1895), Homer, N. Y.
493. Sarah M., b.   ;   "   "   Monson, Mass.

494. George L., b.   ; address, (1895) Worcester, Mass.
495. Emily M., b.   ; address, (1895) Monson, Mass.
496. Alfred J., b.   : address, (1895) Los Angeles, Cal.

VI. CAROLINE (291), second child of Aaron (146), and Sophia, his wife, was born May 17, 1804, in Brooklyn, Conn.; married in Southbridge, Mass., Dec. 1, 1824, Silas Gilmore, of Monson, Mass. She died   , 1875, in Worcester, Mass.; buried in Southbridge. He was born Aug. 5, 1800; died May 5, 1840.

Children.

497. Edwin Oscar, b. Oct. 28, 1825; d. Sept. 27, 1884; m. Mar. 30, 1852, Mary F—— Weld. No issue.
498. Mary Ann, b. July 15, 1827; d. Dec. 19, 1830.
499. Silas Prince, b. Mar. 10, 1829; d. Mar. 23, 1829.
500. Julia Frances, b. Apr. 11, 1832; d. Jan. 17, 1877; m.   , Austin Sterns, in Charlton, Mass.; one dau., Lizzie Frances, b. Sept. 23, 1855, in Southbridge, Mass.; now (1895) living in Worcester, Mass.
501. Henry Sullivan, b. Sept. 3, 1834; m. June 20, 1861, Sarah A—— Hartshorn; he resides in Webster, Mass., (1898) and is the only one of the family living.
502. Caroline Luvan, b. Feb. 5, 1837; d. Nov. 22, 1885; m. Nov. 22, 1869, Henry Aiken.
503. Georgiana, b. July 5, 1839; d. Mar. 20, 1860.

VI. LOUISA (292), third child of Aaron (146), and Sophia, his wife, was born Mar. 15, 1806, in Brooklyn, Conn.; died in Southbridge, Mass., Feb. 1, 1884, aged 78 years; married there Apr. 6, 1826, Sullivan Stone. He was born   ; died Aug. 17, 1861; buried in Southbridge. He was a blacksmith, and gave up his business to his son the spring before he died.

Children.

504. Caroline M——, b. June 21, 1826; d. Apr. 21, 1841.
505. George Sullivan, b. Jan. 12, 1828; d. Feb. 11, 1890.
506. Eliza M——, b. Dec. 20, 1832; is now (1895) living in North Attleboro, Mass. (Mrs. McCambridge.)

VI. FANNY TUCKER (295), sixth child of Aaron (146), and Sophia, his wife, was born Mar. 14, 1815, in Dudley, Mass.; married Dec. 9, 1839, in Southbridge, Mass., by Rev. Eber Carpenter, James R—— Young. Their present address is No. 25 Grant St., Springfield, Mass.

Children.

507. Frank Ripley, b. Apr. 14, 1841, in Southbridge; present address is Springfield, Mass.
508. Aaron Prince, b. Dec. 2, 1842, in Southbridge; d. May 29, 1871, in Springfield.
509. Linus Childs, b. May 9, 1845, in Southbridge; is now (1895) living in Chicago, Ill.

Above children were all married.

VI. DELL SOPHIA (296), seventh child of Aaron (146), and Sophia, his wife, was born in Monson, Mass., June 26, 1820; died Jan. 16, 1847, aged 27 years; buried in Southbridge, Mass; married there Oct. 12, 1840, Merrick Barnes. He was born   ; died——.

Children.

510. Charles Merrick, b. Aug. 21, 1841, in Southbridge; d. Mar. 8, 1865, aged 23 years, 6 months, 18 days.
511. Frank Paine, b. June 10, 1843, in Southbridge; d. Aug. 10, 1843, aged 2 months.
512. Annie, b.   , in Ware, Mass.; d   , in Dudley, Mass.; m.   , —— Edmunds.

VI. MILLY N. (297), first child of Willard (147), by first wife, was born Apr. 27, 1812, in Thompson, Conn.; married Oct. 25, 1838, Addison Pierce, of Jaffrey, N. H. He was born   ; died Mar. 31, 1888, in East Jaffrey, N. H., where his widow now lives.

Children.

513. Myron L——, b. Aug. 3, 1840; d. Sept. 9, 1842.
514. Addison, b. Sept. 8, 1844; m.   ,———; no children.
515. Caroline, b. Mar. 8, 1847; d. May 8, 1855.
516. Clark M——, b. Jan. 18, 1853; m.   , ————; four children. His address is East Jaffrey, N. H.
517. Carrie E——, b. Jan. 9, 1855.

VI. HARVEY (307), first child of Orland (149), by first wife, Rebecca, was born in Dudley, Mass., Oct. 3, 1810; lived, died and was buried there; married ——— Vinton, of Dudley. Was a stone cutter. No issue.

VI. HORACE (308), second child of Orland (149), by first wife, was born Feb. 27, 1812, in Dudley, Mass. Lived for a time in Charlton, Mass., but probably married in Dudley,—first,   , Hannah Rogers, a sister of the second wife of his father, Orland; she died Aug. 20, 1850. He married second, Mar. 5, 1851, Emeline Vinton, of Dudley. No issue by second wife. Horace soon after his second marriage, removed to Dudley, where he died   , 1872. His wife, Emeline, returned to Charlton, and died there Jan. 16, 1875. Horace was buried in Southbridge.

Children.

518. Mary Elizabeth, b. Jan. 27, 1840; is single. P. O. address, 1896, West Dudley, Mass.
519. Charles H——, b. Sept. 29, 1841; d. Feb. 16, 1844; is buried in Charlton, Mass

VI. ELLIOTT (310), fourth child of Orland (149), by first wife, was born in Dudley, Mass., May 8, 1816; d. Aug. 7, 1886, in Charlton, Mass., where he had lived a long time; was a stone cutter; was buried in Charlton Center. Married first, Harriet McIntyre, of Charlton. She died Aug. 31, 1853. He married second, Mar. 28, 1855, Emma Williams, a widow, of   She died Dec. 6, 1883, without issue.

Children by First Wife.

520. William H———, b. June 14, 1841.
521. Martha Maria, b. Apr. 22, 1843.
522. George Elliott, b. Feb. 9, 1847; m.   ; no issue.
523. Rebecca Harriet, b. May 24, 1849; single; lives in Providence, R. I., at 75 Updike St.

VI. LUCIAN (312), sixth child of Orland (149), by first wife, was born Mar. 31, 1820, in Dudley, Mass ; later lived in Worcester; married first,   , ——— Tuttle, of Maine; married second, Elsie ———. He died   , in Holliston, Middlesex Co., Mass.; buried there. The widow now (1896) lives with her son, David. P. O. address, 10 Cutler St., Worcester, Mass.

Children.

524. Alice Maria, b. in Holliston, Mass., June 8, 1851; m. at Worcester, Mass., Oct. 2, 1871, Edward Lovell, a shoemaker. She died in Keene, N. H., Aug. 7, 1872
525. David Lucian, b. Apr. 16, 1853, in Holliston, Mass.
526. Hattie Rebecca, b July 8, 1854, in Worcester; d. July 11, 1872.
527. Willie Harvey, b. Nov. 5, 1855, in Worcester; d. May 27, 1864.

VI. DAVID (313), seventh child of Orland (149), was born in Dudley, Mass., Mar. 1, 1822; died Sept. 17, 1873; buried in Providence, R. I.; married   , 1859. Jennie Belle, of Philadelphia, Penn., where he lived.

Children.

528. Carrie, b.
529. Jennie, b.
530. Ella, b.
531. May, b.   , in Philadelphia.
532. Daisy, b.   , in Providence.

Will any one inform me where the above children may be found? [Author.]

VI. CAROLINE (314), eighth child of Orland (149), was born in Southbridge, Mass., June 7, 1824; married Apr. 11, 1848, in Providence, R. I., by Rev. Mr. Bradford, James F. Potter, of Plainfield, Conn., who was born there Sept. 2, 1823. Present P. O. address, No. 17 North Pleasant St., Taunton, Mass.

Children.

533. Charles J——, b. Jan. 6, 1859, in Plainfield, Conn.; d. Feb. 10, 1864, at Taunton, Mass.; buried in Plainfield.
534. Frank E——, b. Feb. 1, 1864, in Taunton, Mass.

VI. ALMIRA (315), ninth child of Orland (149), was born in Southbridge, Mass., July 29, 1826; married May 15, 1848, in Providence, R. I., Horace Edwards   Present P. O. address: 50 Point St., Providence, R. I.

Children.

535. Emily A., b. June 18, 1850; d. Apr. 4, 1856.
536. Horace P., b. Aug. 31, 1854; d. Sept. 24, 1862.
537. David G——, b. Mar. 3, 1856, in Providence. P. O. address: 133-7 Point St., Providence, R. I.
538. Amy A——, b. Apr. 26, 1858.

VI. SARAH JANE (319), thirteenth child of Orland (149), by second wife, was born Dec. 19, 1837; married Mar. 6, 1860, George M—— Frost, of Charlton, Mass., where they now (1895) reside.

Children.

539. Adaline S——, b. Nov. 30, 1862, in Charlton, Mass.
540. Charles E——, b. Dec. 7, 1864; d. Mar. 25, 1882, in Charlton.
541. Carrie E——, b. Mar. 25, 1867, in Charlton.
542. George W——, b. Jan. 28, 1869, in Charlton.
543. Sarah Gertrude, b. July 25, 1875, in Charlton.

Note: According to the "History of Oxford, Mass.," by George F. Daniels, the Princes of that place were quite numerous, and were descendants of David, of Sutton, Mass.

VI. LINUS (320), son by second wife of Orland, (149), was born Feb. 12, 1840, in Charlton, Mass.; married Apr. 8, 1865, Mrs. Addie Carpenter, (maiden name, Hill). Since marriage they have lived in other towns. Their present address is Charlton City, Mass.

Children.

544. Rose E——, b. Jan. 13, 1866, in Charlton; m. Nov. 15, 1883, Edward M. Bowers, of Charlton.
545. Nellie, b.   ; no record of birth in Charlton; m.   , Horace B. Sinclair.
546. Luella, b. May 14, 1874, in Charlton; m.   , Charles Bowen.
547. Emenette, b. Oct. 24, 1876, in Charlton; m.   , Fred Dempsey.
548. Florence, b.   ; no record of birth in Charlton.

VI. VERNON (321), son by second wife of Orland (149), was born Dec. 21, 1843; married in Worcester, Mass., Apr. 16, 1870, by Rev. M. Richardson, Sarah M.

Rogers, of East Woodstock, Conn. Vernon went to Worcester to live in 1868. Is a carpenter. Address: No. 3 South Winfield St., Worcester, Mass. (1895).

Children.

549. Edward Wesley, b. Oct. 1, 1871; d. Nov. 25, 1871.
550. George Vernon, b. June 11, 1875.
551. Herbert Eugene, b. Nov. 18, 1878.
552. Sadie Mabel, b. Jan. 31, 1887.

VI. CHARLES HENRY (322), last child of Orland (149), and by second wife, Adeline (Rogers), was born Jan. 15, 1849, in Charlton, Mass.; married Jan. 15, 1876, Emily F—— Robbins, of that place. No issue. Both living. P. O. address, Charlton City, Mass.

VI. TIMOTHY (334), second child of Joseph (154), was born in Brooklyn, Conn., Apr. 18, 1821; married ———; Julia ———. She died July 6, 1849, aged 25 years.

Children.

553. Catherine, b. Aug. 1, 1845; d. Aug. 20, 1845.
554. Lucy H., b. Mar. 26, 1847.

VI. DAVID (339), first child of David (156), was born June 21, 1816, in Brooklyn, Conn.; died in Jacksonville, Ill., Dec. 19, 1889, of acute pneumonia; married first in Baltimore, Md., Nov. 25, 1841, Mary Jane Dawson, by whom he had four children, all of whom died young; married second, in Fredonia, N. Y., Lucy Manning Chandler, who was born April 1, 1828, in Skancatles, N. Y., and who was the first of three children of John and Mary (Manning) Chandler, of Pomfret, Conn. It is worthy of note that Lucy Manning (Chandler) Prince, was by the Abbot and Chandler published genealogies, the sixth cousin as well as sister-in-law of her husband, Dr. David Prince.

VII. JAMES MOULTON (353), second child of (188), was born Dec. 8, 1828, in Oxford, Mass.; married first, May 1, 1851, in Douglas, Mass., Sarah J. Titus, who was born Aug. 18, 1828, in Sutton, Mass., and died Sept. 26, 1871, in Webster, Mass., aged 43 years, 1 month, 8 days; married second, Feb. 5, 1872, Lucella W. Stone, of Oxford, who was born Nov. 19, 1839, and died July 24, 1892, without issue; married third, Oct. 26, 1893, Allura Gibson, born Nov. 30, 1860, in Sutton. Present P. O. address: Box 48, Webster, Mass.

Children by First Wife.

555. Clara Jeannette, b. July 11, 1854, in Worcester. Unmarried.
556. Benjamin Moulton, b. Jan. 9, 1856, in Worcester; married Lillian Flora Bixby.

VII. LEWIS S., (370), first child of David (193), was born Jan 19, 1838; died June 11, 1881, in Webster, Mass., and buried there; married Aug. 12, 1868, Mrs. Mary Merritt, (maiden name Sutherland) of Glasgow, Scotland. He was a soldier in the Civil War, 51st Mass. Reg't.

VII SARAH JANE (371), second child of David (193), was born May 3, 1842; married , William Walker, of Brookfield, Mass. She died July 12, 1868.

VII. GEORGIANNA (374), fifth child of David (193), was born in Webster, Mass., Sept. 6, 1849; married June 6, 1865, by Rev. John A. Buckingham, of Sturbridge, Mass., Warren A. Walker, who was born in Brookfield, Mass., Sept. 2, 1839. P. O. address (1895): 51 Belmont St., Worcester, Mass.

Children.

557. Hattie L., b. Feb. 28, 1866.
558. Charles F., b. Feb. 7, 1868.

559. Ida J., b. Aug. 14, 1872; m. Nov. 19, 1894, Edward E. Buxton, of Worcester, Mass.
560. David H., b. Mar. 7, 1873; d. Mar. 8, 1873.
561. Florence A., b. Dec. 17, 1881; d. Aug. 7, 1882.
562. Bessie A., b. June 20, 1883.

First four children born in Brookfield, Mass.; last two born in Worcester.

VII. HENRY S. (375), sixth child of David (193), was born in Webster, Mass., Nov. 6, 1854; married July 7, 1878, by Rev. —— Sleeper, of Worcester, Amanda Rand, of that place. She was born about 1856-7.

P. O. address: 24 Columbia St., Greenbush, Albany, N. Y. (1895).

Children.

563. Eva S., b. Oct. 24, 1879.
564. Clifton H., b. Sept. 12, 1881.
565. Gracy N., b. Dec. 15, 1882; d. Aug. 8, 1883.
566. David L., b. Dec. 1, 1883.
567. Ray C., b. July 14, 1889.

Above children born in Worcester, Mass.

VII. EMILY (396), first child of Lyman (205), was born in Thompson, Conn., Jan. 2, 1811; married May 3, 1837, Anson Barrett, a carpenter by trade; settled in North Woodstock, Conn. He died there July 27, 1890. She now lives there. (1895.)

Children.

568. Ellen, b. Apr. 29, 1838; m. Mar. 7, 1872, Augustus Johnson.
569. Smith, b. Oct. 31, 1840; m. Feb. 15, 1870, Emma Hill, of Willimantic, Conn.
570. Mary, b. May 3, 18—; d. ——

571. William Marsh, b. Sept. 16, 1847; m. Oct. 11, 1893, Miss Lucy O. Lombard, of North Woodstock, Conn.; settled there.
572. Mary, b. Oct. 26, 1851; m. Feb. 9, 1877, Henry L. Burt (Druggist); settled in Putnam, Conn., and now lives there (1899).

VII. LOREN (398), third child of Lyman (205), was born in Thompson, Conn., about Mar. 7, 1821; married about 1842, Amanda Barnes, of Sutton, Mass., daughter of William Barnes. She died   ; buried in Uxbridge, Mass. He is at present living on the Town farm at Thompson, Conn. (1897).

Children.

573. William Henry, b.   ; m.
574. Nellie, b.   ; m.
575. Lilla, b.   ; m.

Children's names obtained from Loren, who alone is responsible.

VII. JEROME (400), first child of George (207), was born in Woonsocket, R. I., May 28, 1842; married first,   , 1868, in Uxbridge, Mass., Maria L. McDonald; married second, Nov. 7, 1877, in Milford, Mass., Melissa A. Fisk.

He enlisted three times. First, Co. H, 15th Reg't, Mass. Vols. He served till close of the war. See F. A. Prince's "War Records of Our Ancestors." Is at present at the Soldiers' Home, Chelsea, Mass.

P. O. address of family (1897): 32 South Main St., Milford, Mass.

Child by First Wife.

576. George F., b. June 8, 1869; lives with Mrs. Jerome Prince, unmarried. (1899).

Children by Second Wife.

577. Nellie M., b. Mar. 16, 1879.
578. Lilla B., b. Jan. 10, 1885.

VII. MARY OPHELIA (417), first child of Albert (221), and Ophelia (Elliott) Prince, was born in Thompson, Conn., Oct. 9, 1845; married Mar. 11, 1860, at home, by Rev. —— Brown, of North Woodstock, Conn., Allen Barber Richmond, who was then of Thompson. He was an overseer in the Grosvenordale Co.'s mill, at Grosvenordale, Conn., for a long time, and is now (1898) living in New York state. She is at present (1899) living at New Boston, Conn. No issue.

VII. FRANCIS ALBERT (418), second child of Albert (221), and Ophelia (Elliott) Prince, was born in Thompson, Conn., May 15, 1851, at the home of his grandfather, (Nathan) where his parents then resided. When seven years of age, his father moved to East Woodstock, and there he attended school in the Paine district. At the age of fourteen he was sent to the Nichols Academy, at Dudley, Mass., where he spent three years in a school which was classed at that time as the best school for thorough training and good discipline to be found in New England. At the age of eighteen he served as an apprentice with Dexter May, at Dudley, as a carpenter, after which he obtained a situation in Southbridge, Mass. Not liking the location, he went to Worcester, Mass., and obtained a very desirable position with ˙Dea. Ward, then a very heavy and prosperous contractor. After staying one year with Dea. Ward, he again had a better position offered him near to his birth-place, (North Grosvenordale) where extensive changes were to be made in getting ready for the building of one of the largest mills in New England, together with one hundred tenements. While there he was married, May 30, 1872, at the parsonage of the Rev. Jabez Pack, in East Woodstock, to Sarah Maria Chaffee. She was born Jan. 31, 1847, in Southbridge, Mass.; afterward moved

RESIDENCE OF FRANK A. PRINCE,
21 MAIN ST. DANIELSON, CONN.

with her parents to Thompson, Conn.; was the first of three children of Charles and Sarah Elizabeth Chaffee. Mr. and Mrs. Prince, subsequent to their marriage, lived in North Grosvenordale about three years, removing from there to Perryville, Mass., and after staying there two years removed to Danielsonville, (now Danielson) Conn., where he built for himself a residence on Mechanics St. Later he purchased the fine residence where he now resides. In 1880 he assumed charge of the wood shop of the Quinebaug Co., which position he has held for nineteen years. In 1888 he was elected a Burgess of the Borough, which position he held for three years, and again in 1893, was elected to the same position. In 1892 the town of Brooklyn elected him as second Selectman, which position he filled with such general satisfaction that he was again elected in 1894, again in 1895, and still again in 1896, thus serving the town four years as its Selectman.

Children.

579. Charles Henry, b. in Thompson, Conn., Sept. 7, 1873; m. Annie Bell Bright.

580. Nathan Dyer, b. in Danielson, Conn., Dec. 1, 1878; is a graduate of Killingly High school, class of '98; a popular teacher on the banjo, guitar and mandolin; also holds a position in the Windham County National Bank of Danielsonville; resides with his parents at the above place (1899).

On May 30, 1897, Mr. and Mrs. F. A. Prince celebrated their silver wedding anniversary, and among the many beautiful tokens of remembrance from their many friends is the following from their oldest son. It was entirely unexpected, and the manner in which it was read added so much effectiveness to the occasion that it brought tears to many eyes. Following we give it in full:

LINES

On the Silver Wedding Anniversary of Mr. and Mrs. F. A. PRINCE, May 30, '97, composed by Charles H. Prince, and affectionately dedicated

To Father and Mother.

DEAR PARENTS AND FRIENDS:

I ask you for a moment to listen
   To one who is sincere,
Who wishes blessings to attend
   Through all your life's career.

Today we have assembled
   Our kind esteem to pay,
To you who have been united
   In fighting life's untried way.

Not in "single blessedness,"
   But happily together,
Have you faced the fight victoriously
   Through changing wind and weather.

So we come today with greetings,
   With merry hearts and true,
To show the kindly feelings
   That time hath won for you.

The twenty-five years have swiftly passed
   From the day of your marriage date—
A day historic in our land,
   Sad in our country's fate.

And now o'er the years that have vanished
   Let us pause for a moment to gaze;
If life hath had some trials,
   It must have had pleasant ways.

SARAH MARIA (CHAFFEE) PRINCE.
PAGE 98.

Perhaps a bit of the story
  Of how it all came about,
Might be of interest to some of you
  Who now are in much doubt.

Years ago in Woodstock town,
  Nestling among the hills,
Fed by the produce of farm lands,
  Nourished by Nature's rills,

Lived, not a mile from each other,
  A youth and maiden fair,
He of the Princes loyal,
  She of the debonair.

Time works out its changes;
  Cupid was never still
Till out from the thrifty farmlands,
  Out from over the hill

He brought the youth and maiden,
  Now grown to riper years,
And drove them toward the parson's,
  Free from all cares and fears.

Straight to the dominie's house they went;
  Bright shining was the sun,
And brighter still their faces
  After the deed was done.

Fair were the plans and castles
  Builded then in air;
They seemed to you all so real
  And free from every care.

And sweet mem'ries still you cherish
  Of the days that are no more,
But the future is still brighter
  For the burdens pressing sore.

Two sons have come to lighten
    And help you in the fight;
Though the elder one has left you,
    He feels your watchful sight.

The younger son, who's still at home,
    I trust will always be
A blessing to you, till at length
    He leaves the paternal tree.

And what if there's silver in your hair
    Which soon will turn to gray!
We are not blind to what it means—
    You cannot always stay.

Beauty will faint, and fade, and die,
    Only leaving a light behind,
But as it fades and moments fly
    The calmer grows the mind.

And may the love that now cements,
    Your happy hearts as one,
Grow deeper, sweeter, as the years
    Roll onward, one by one.

May the path you walk be strewn with flowers,
    Through every changing scene,
And may adversity's dread hours
    Be few and far between.

A veil that hangs before our eyes
    Keeps future years concealed,
But in yon distant, blissful heaven
    To God they stand revealed.

As He thro' paths of grief or joy
    Conducts you as His own,
May you in every changing scene
    Say, "Lord, Thy will be done."

Your golden wedding may you reach,
    Though distant it appears,
No memory of a word or deed
    To dim your eyes with tears.

Surrounded then by loving friends
    And all that life endears,
Give those a thought who then shall be
    Within the eternal years.

For some who stand beside you now
    The coming years to greet,
Will not be there to celebrate
    That day so fair and sweet.

Will not? How do we know but then,
    More lovingly than now,
Unseen, unfelt, their lips shall rain
    Love tokens on your brow?

And when our earthly lives shall close,
    And dust to dust be given,
May we all here together walk
    The golden streets of heaven.

Franklin, Mass., May 26, 1897.

VII. JERUSHA JACOBS (419), third child of Albert (221), and Ophelia (Elliott) Prince, was born May 12, 1856, in Thompson, Conn.; married May 2, 1875, in Webster, Mass., at the parsonage, by Rev. T. T. Filmer, Edward Francois Richardson, who was born, . She lives at present (1899) in Worcester, Mass.

Children.

581.   Arthur Francois, b. Dec. 25, 1875, in Webster, Mass.; d. Sept. 4, 1876, in Webster, of cholera infantum; buried in Wilsonville, Conn.

582. Lillian Rosamond, b. Dec. 10, 1876, in Webster; d. Aug. 6, 1877, in Webster, of cholera infantum; buried in Wilsonville, Conn.
583. Louis Earnest, b. July 5, 1878, in Worcester, Mass.; m. Apr. 28, 1897, by Rev. Henry Brown, at Warren, R. I., Lena Brown, formerly of Danielson, Conn., dau. of E nmons Brown. They have one child—Bertha Carroll, b. Feb. 10, 1898.

VII. EMILY MARILLA (435), only child of Daniel and Emily (Carpenter) Prince, was born Aug. 31, 1844, in Dudley, Mass.; married there Oct. 27, 1868, by Rev. J. G. Sanger, (Universalist) Edwin Freeman Bradford, first child of William and Caroline (Cummings) Bradford. He was born Apr. 27, 1841, in Southbridge, Mass., and was a farmer boy. About 1855 the family moved to Dudley for better facilities of education; about three years after this the mother died, and the children were scattered. E. F. Bradford started for himself; taught school in Charlton, Mass., and Thompson, Conn., and finished his education at the Nichols Academy in Dudley. He then went to an uncle (Henry Bradford) in Nashua, N. H., and studied telegraphy, thence went to Kewanee, Ill., as clerk in C. B. & Q. R. R. office there; thence to Kirkwood, Ill., as telegraph operator. (About one year in each place). From Kirkwood he went to Macomb for sixteen years as R. R. Agt. In Apr. 1881, went to Hannibal, Mo., as Gen. Agt. About 1888 went to Quincy, Ill., and has been the Gen. Agt. of the C. B. & Q. R. R. at that point ever since, and is a trusted and efficient officer, and an obliging and universally popular citizen.

Children.

584. Caroline, b. Apr. 15, 1870.
585. Madora, b. Aug. 3, 1871; m. at Quincy, Ill., Mar. 20, 1895, Allen Francis Moore.

NATHAN DYER PRINCE.
PAGE 90. NUMBER 586.

586. Fannie Louise, b. Oct. , 1873.
587. Bertha Pamele, b. July 9, 1880.

Above children all born in Iacomb.

VII. JOHN DUDLEY (436), son of John Whitney (234), was born July 1, 1870; m. in Thompson, Conn., May 3, 1892, Lillian Barnes, of New Boston, Conn.

Children.

588. John Earl, b Dec. 12 1892.

VII. BERTHA MAY (451), first child of John Adams, by second wife, Charlotte, was born in Worcester, Mass., Sept. 7, 1869; married Wednesday, Aug. 18, 1897, at home, (Prospect Farm) in Leicester, Mass., by Rev. Alonzo Sanderson, of Worcester, to J. G. Schmohl, who was Mayor of Galena, Ill., and is also an extensive dealer in agricultural and electrical supplies.

VII. HENRY ROOTES JACKSON (461), third child of Oliver Hillhouse (265), was born Nov. 15, 1859; married Apr. , 1884, Maria Jane, eldest daughter of John and Mary Turley. She was born,———.

Children.

589. Oliver Hillhouse, b. July 14, 1886.
590. Basil, b. Jan. 6, 1889.
591. Florence Turley, b. Jan. 5, 1891.
592. Francis, b. Sept. 5, 1893.

VII. MARIA JACQUELINE (462), fourth child of Oliver Hillhouse (265), was born Nov. 10, 1861; married April 29, 1884, Jordan Sumner Thomas, youngest son of William George and Mary (Sumner) Thomas of Wilmington, N. C.

Family live in Brunswick, Ga.

Children.

593. Florence, b. May 29, 1885.
594. Mary Sumner, b. Dec. 1, 1886; d. Sept. 28, 1887, of cholera infantum.
595. William George, b. Jan. 13, 1889.
596. Sarah Prince, b. Dec. 4, 1890.
597. Marie Jacqueline, b. Oct. 18, 1892.

VII. VIRGINIA SELINA GREEN (468), was born July 9, 1855; married Feb. 21, 1882, William Ashe Poe, of Macon, Ga. (A cousin of Edgar Allen Poe, the poet). W. A. Poe was the son of Hon. Washington Poe, who died Oct. 1, 1836, and Selina Shirley. She still lives, with all her faculties, at the age of 82 years.

Children.

598. Harvey Hillhouse, b. Nov. 21, 1882.
599. Shirley, b. Oct. 22, 1884.
600. Sarah Virginia, b. Mar. 15, 1888.
601. Willie, b. Oct. 28, 1890.
602. Edgar Allen, b. Nov. 28, 1893.

Above children all born in Macon, Ga.

VII. WILLIAM S. (474), first child of Sanford and Sophia (Carr) Prince, was born Sept. 20, 1820; died Feb. 3, 1890; married Apr. 5, 1845, Jane Hill. She is living at this date (Mar., 1897).

Children.

603. John S., b. Sept. 15, 1846. P. O. address: Hurleyville, Sullivan Co., N. Y.
604. Alice, b. Jan. 17, 1849. P. O. address: Bushville, Sullivan Co., N. Y.
605. Robert H., b. Nov. 7, 1851.
606. Wilber Joseph, b. Apr. 14, 1856. P. O. address: Hurleyville, N. Y.

607. George E., b. Jan. 1, 1861. P. O. address: Hurleyville, N. Y.
608. Leona, b.   ; m.
609. Luella, b. Aug. 15, 1867. P. O. address: New York City, N. Y.

Above children all married.

VII. ORRIN (475), second child of Sanford and Sophia (Carr) Prince, was born Apr. 19, 1822; married   , 1855; died   , 1868, in Sullivan Co., N. Y.

Children.

610. Millard F., b.   ; m.   . He is at present of the firm of M. F. Prince & Co., Brokerage and Commission. Canned goods department is 105 Hudson St. Sugar department, 102 Wall St., New York City.

VII. JOHN M. (476), third child of Sanford and Sophia (Carr) Prince, was born June 20, 1824; married Mar. 31, 1852, Elizabeth J. Kinne.

P. O. address (1896): Liberty Falls, N. Y.

Children.

611. Jamie, b. Aug. 26, 1855; d. Oct. 15, 1865.
612. Amanda M., b. Apr. 9, 1860; d. Oct. 30, 1865.
613. Walter G , b. Sept. 5, 1866. P. O. address: Liberty, Falls, N. Y.

VII. LAURA S. (477), fourth child of Sanford and Sophia (Carr) Prince, was born May 9, 1828; married,   ; d.   , 1894. Had four children.

VII. ELMIRA J. (478), fifth child of Sanford and Sophia (Carr) Prince, was born Aug. 15, 1831; married,
Had two children.

VII. CAROLINE (479), sixth child of Sanford and Sophia (Carr) Prince, was born Aug. 10, 1836; married, ———; died ———, 1872. Had four children.

VII. JAMES F., (480), seventh child of Sanford and Sophia (Carr) Prince, was born Dec. 1 or 5, 1839; married Dec. 20, 1859, by Rev. M. Coachman, in the town of Liberty, Sullivan Co., N. Y., Mary Adelia Hornbeck. She was born Nov. 28, 1840. They are both living (1897) at Bushville, Sullivan Co., N. Y.

Children.

614. William Sanford, b. Jan. 15, 1861.
615. Clara A., b. Mar. 31, 1863.
616. Catharine J., b. Jan. 1, 1868; d. Oct. 7, 1868.
617. Anna F., b. Sept. 14, 1869.
618. Clarence A., b. Sept. 26, 1873.
619. Melven J., b. Apr. 24, 1882.

Note: Clarence A. not married (1897).

P. O. address of above children: Bushville, N. Y.

VII. MARY E. (481), eighth child of Sanford and Sophia (Carr) Prince, was born ———, 1842; married, ———. Had two children.

VII. SANFORD C. (485), fourth child of Jonathan (270), by first wife, was born in Otto, N. Y., May 17, 1838; married first, Feb. 8, 1863, Martha Jane Ross, of ————, and who was—————. She died Jan. 25, 1873. He married second, Apr. 9, 1874, Sarah E. Davis.

Sanford held many positions of trust, such as Constable, Justice of the Peace, Supervisor, three times chairman of the board, Deputy Sheriff, Notary Public, Postmaster nearly two years,—resigned for better positions; was four times elected Commander of Chas. Green Post, No. 216, Dept. of Wisconsin; was Aide de Camp on Gen. Warren's

Staff, and is now Adjutant of his Post. Was with different railroad companies for nine years,—resigned on account of poor health.

P. O. address (1896): Lynxville, Wis.

See "War Records of Our Ancestors," by F. A. Prince.

Children by First Wife.

620. Ulysses S., b. Nov. 29, 1864; d. Apr. 6, 1865.
621. Edwin L., b. Feb. 5, 1866; living in Lynxville, Wis. (1896).
622. Mary L., b. May 4, 1869; living in Jersey City, N. J.
623. Sanford N., b. July 22, 1871; living in Lynxville, Wis.

Children by Second Wife.

624. John C., b. Jan. 5, 1875; d. Jan. 25, 1875.
625. Henry W., b. Dec. 18, 1875. } Living, 1896.
626. Amy Grace, b. Jan. 23, 1877. }
627. George Dickinson, b. June 5, 1879; d. Mar. 21, 1880.
628. Harley, b. Apr. 23, 1881; d. Jan. 23, 1883.
629. Ella May, b. June 15, 1884; d. Jan. 14, 1890.
630. Nancy Elizabeth, b. Oct. 28, 1887; d. Jan. 15, 1890.
631. Alva Thomas, b. Sept. 22, 1889; living, 1896.

Five of the above children died of diphtheria.

VII. WILLIAM H. (520), first child of Elliott Prince, (310), was born June 14, 1841, in Dudley, Mass. (Now living there, two miles north of Dudley Academy). Married Nov. 29, 1866, in Providence, R. I., by Rev. A. Woodbury, Caroline E—— Green.

Children.

632. Charles Swan, b. in Providence, R. I., Aug. 6, 1870; m.   , Anna M. Thatcher.

VII. MARTHA MARIA (521), second child of Elliott Prince (310), was born April 22, 1843, and now lives in the south-east part of Charlton, Mass.; married June 15, 1869, at Worcester, Mass., by Rev. M. Richardson, Joseph Gilbert Howe. P. O. address: Box 333 Webster, Mass.

Children.

633. Frank Mason, b. Oct. 21, 1875, in Worcester, Mass.

VII. GEORGE ELLIOTT (522), third child of Elliott Prince (310), was born in Charlton, Mass., Feb. 9, 1847; married in same place, Dec. 6, 1873, by Rev. Edward Smiley, Kate Henrietta Putnam, daughter of Russell Putnam, of Webster, Mass. She was born Feb. 11, 1856, and now lives in Webster. He died in Webster, Mar. 2, 1875, without issue, aged 28 years. Buried in Charlton.

VIII. BENJAMIN MOULTON (556), son of James Moulton and Sarah J. (Titus) Prince, was born Jan. 9, 1856, Worcester, Mass.; married Nov. 12, 1878, in Webster, Mass., by Rev. Sanford B. Sweetser, Lillian Flora Bixby, daughter of Henry Bixby. She was born Mar. 12, 1856, in Webster. Present address is No. 12 Riverside St., Worcester, Mass. (1898.)

Children.

634. Walter Everett, b. July 18, 1881, in Norwich, Conn.
635. Ernest Paul, b. July 10, 1891, in Worcester, Mass.
636. Arthur Leslie, b. July 4, 1894, in Worcester, Mass.

VIII. CHARLES HENRY (579), son of F. A. (418), and Sarah M. (Chaffee) Prince, was born in Thompson, Ct., Sept. 7, 1873; married in Franklin, Mass., at the residence of the bride's parents, June 8, 1898, Annie Bell Bright, who was born there, Apr. 14, 1872, and was the third of seven children of Warren Henry and Mary Ellen (Peary) Bright. She is a graduate of Franklin High school, class of '90, and was for nearly five years an efficient and popular teacher in one of the principal schools of the above place. Both Mr. and Mrs. Prince are recognized as being very efficient, earnest, and popular workers in Epworth League and Church affairs. Mr. Prince is a graduate of Killingly High school, at Danielson, Conn., class of '92. After graduating, he served nearly four years with W. H. Hamilton, of Danielson, as a printer, after which he secured a position in Franklin as foreman of the Sentinel Printing office, which position he now holds.

Children.

VIII. JOHN S. (603), son of William S. and Jane (Hill) Prince, was born Sept. 15, 1846; married Feb. 17, 1875, Ella J. Mitteer. P. O. address (1897): Hurleyville, Sullivan Co., N. Y.

Children.

637. William M., b. Feb. 29, 1880.

VIII. WILBER J. (606), son of William S. and Jane (Hill) Prince, was born Apr. 14, 1856; married Jan. 27, 1881, Jennie E. Hill. P. O. address (1897): Hurleyville, Sullivan Co., N. Y.

Children.

638. Leslie H., b. Feb. 1, 1884

VIII. GEORGE E. (607), son of William S. and Jane (Hill) Prince, was born Jan. 1, 1861; married Mar. 16, 1881, Mattie Sharrock. P. O. address (1897): Hurleyville, Sullivan Co., N. Y.

Children.

639. Evie, b. Dec. 17, 1881.
640. Ethel, b. Aug. 6, 1890.
641. Gladys, b. Sept. 11, 1895.

VIII. WILLIAM SANFORD (614), son of James F. and Mary Adelia (Hornbeck) Prince, was born Jan. 15, 1861; married Nov. 6, 1889, Rose E. Sturdevant.

Children.

642. Eva M., b. Dec. 6, 1894.

VIII. CLARA A. (615), daughter of James F. and Mary Adelia (Hornbeck) Prince, was born Mar. 31, 1863 in Bushville, Sullivan Co., N. Y; married Dec. 6, 1881, Isaac M. Harris. He was born Feb. 5, 1857. P. O. address: Bushville, Sullivan Co., N. Y. (1898).

Children.

643. Nora A., b. Mar. 16, 1883.
644. Fred G., b. Aug. 4, 1885.
645. Jay B., b. July 25, 1889.
646. Elmer R., b. Dec. 12, 1894.

VIII. ANNA F. (617), fourth child of James F. and Mary Adelia (Hornbeck) Prince, was born Sept. 14, 1869; married Nov. 20, 1889, Herbert S. Palmer.

Children.

647. Flora, b. Dec. 24, 1891.

CHARLES HENRY PRINCE.
PAGE 110. NUMBER 579.

ANNIE BELL (BRIGHT) PRINCE.
PAGE 110.

VIII. CHARLES SWAN, (632), son of William H. and Caroline E. (Green) Prince, was born in Providence, R. I., Aug. 6, 1870; married Sept. 8, 1892, by Rev. S. Thatcher, Anne M——Thatcher, of Warrenville, Windham Co., Conn. She died Jan. 11, 1895, in Webster, Mass., where he now lives.

Children.

648. Paul Bradford, b. Jan. 10, 1895.

~~~~~~~~~~

The following in regard to Thompson's first ministers may be interesting to some of the descendants whose ancestors were married by Thompson ministers:

REV. MARSTON CABOT was ordained pastor of the First Church in Thompson, Conn., Feb. 5, 1730, and filled that position until April, 1756. covering a period of twenty-six years of faithful service, during which time eight hundred and thirty infants were baptized by him.

REV. NOADIAH RUSSELL was ordained Nov. 9, 1757, faithfully serving until 1795. Nine hundred and twenty-six children were baptized by him during his ministry.

REV. DANIEL DOW was ordained April 20, 1796, serving until 1849.

The noticeable feature is that the pastorates of the first three preachers of Thompson First Church covered a period of one hundred and nineteen years.

RECORDS OF OTHER PRINCE FAMILIES.

The Author believes the following to be on line of Robert Prince, of Salem, Mass., rather than tradition, which says that John Prince settled in New York state. Married, but nothing further known other than that he had two sons.

Children.

2. Samuel, b.   ; m.
3. Robert, b.   ; m.

II. ROBERT, (3), married Mary Burgess; no date given.

Children.

4. Mary, b.   ; m.   , David Phillips.
5. William, b.   ; m.   , Ann Thorne.
6. Elizabeth, b.   ; m.
7. Samuel, b.   ; m.   , Ruth Carman.
8. Robert, b.   ; d. young.
9. Susannah, b.   ; m.   , Mr. Montross.

III. SAMUEL, (7), born in New York, 1727; married in New York, 1754, Ruth Carman, who was born in New York, 1729. He was a soldier in the Revolutionary war, and fought gallantly for his country.

Note: The name Samuel Prince has not been found on the Rolls on file in Record and Pension Office, War Department, Washington, D. C., in service of any New York organization during the War of the Revolution.

Children.

10. Elizabeth, b.   , 1755, in New York; d.   , 1851, aged 96 years; m.   , Gabriel Winter.
11. Sarah, b.   , 1757; d. of cancer,—no date.
12. Ruth, b.   , 1759; d. Feb.   , 1814; m   , 1776, Nicholas B. Brower.
13. Samuel Jr., b. May 29, 1762; m. Nov. 5, 1785, Mary Norwood.

IV. SAMUEL JR., (13), was born May 29, 1762, in New York; died May 23, 1839, in Bridge St., Brooklyn, N. Y.; married Nov. 5, 1785, Mary Norwood. She was born Sept. 14, 1768; died Apr. 15, 1845, in Bridge St., Brooklyn, N. Y. Samuel, Jr., was a soldier in the War of 1812; was taken prisoner by the British and went to the Elizabeth, N. J., prison, which was called the "Old Sugar House." He was afterwards exchanged with other prisoners.

The Record and Pension Office, War Department, Washington, D. C., show that Samuel Prince served as a private in Captain Earl Fillmore's company, 157th New York Volunteers (with a detachment of the 157th and 131st Regiment New York Volunteers, Lieutenant Colonel Caleb Clark commanding), War of 1812. His name appears on the records with remarks as follows: "Commencement of service, March 10, 1813. Expiration of service, March 25, 1813. Term charged, 16 days."

The records further show that S. Prince, Jr., served as a Corporal and a Sergeant in Captain Tunis B. Van Brunt's company, Forbes' battalion of artillery, New York, War of 1812. The muster roll from September 2, 1814, to December 3, 1814, bears remarks as follows concerning him: "Commencement of service, September 2, 1814. Expiration of service, December 3, 1814. Term charged, 3 months and 2 days."

No further information relative to the service of Samuel Prince has been found of Record.

By authority of the SECRETARY OF WAR.

RECORDS OF OTHER PRINCE FAMILIES.

Children.

14. Mary, b. Aug. 8, 1786.
15. Samuel, Jr., b. July 20, 1788.
16. William Augustus, b. Nov. 24, 1790.
17. Eliza, b. Dec. 2, 1792.
18. Sarah, b. June 20, 1794; d. Aug. 10, 1795.
19. Sarah, b. Mar. 4, 1796.
20. Robert, b. Jan. 20, 1798; d. Nov. 22, 1870.
21. Margaret, b. Nov. 20, 1800.
22. Benjamin, b. July 27, 1803.
23. Harriet, b. Nov. 22, 1805.
24. Edward, b. June 6, 1807.
25. Infant, boy, b. Feb. 27, 1809; d. at birth.
26. George Washington, b. Feb. 25, 1811.

V. ROBERT, (20), was born Jan. 20, 1798; died Nov. 22, 1870; married first, Miss Moore, date unknown; married second, Oct. 12, 1835, Antoinette Cargill, who was born Oct. 18, 1816, and died Nov. , 1859; married third time, Mary Elizabeth Adams, (formerly Cargill), Jan. 13, 1862. She died,——.

Child by First Wife.

27. Infant, boy, d. young, mother and child dying same time shortly after birth.

Children by Second Wife.

28. David, b. Sept. 5, 1836; m. , Frances A. Comins.
29. Mary M., b. Dec. 12, 1838; m. Sept. 5, 1860, Albert R. Bass.
30. Samuel, b. Apr. 18, 1840; d. Oct. , 1854.
31. Robert Jr., b. Dec. 6, 1841; m. , Sadie Ten Eyck.
32. Abraham C., b. Sept. 8, 1844; m. , Lizzie F. Lovejoy.
33. Antoinette, b. Sept 19, 1846; m. , Alexander Bass.

34. James G., b. Sept. 9, 1849; d. about 1881 or 2.
35. Adelaide B., b. Oct. 21, 1851; d. about 1854.
36. Alfred B., b. Aug. 9, 1854; d.

Child by Third Wife.

37. Adelaide, b.   , 1863; d.   , 1864, aged 1 year and 1 month.

VI. DAVID, (28), was born Sept. 5, 1836; married June 13, 1860, Frances A. Comins. She was daughter of John P. Comins, who lived for many years on a farm about one and one-half miles south-west of Danielson, Conn. David Prince is secretary and treasurer of the Prince Manufacturing Co., incorporated April 28, 1879, No. 71 Maiden Lane, New York, N. Y. Works at Bowman's, Prince P. O., Carbon county, Penn. Manufacturers of Prince's Metallic Paint and Mineral Brown.

Children.

38. Frederick A., b. Mar. 26, 1861; d. Apr. 10, 1863.
39. Adelaide, b. Nov. 1, 1862; m. Sept. 5, 1882, Ellis P. Earle.
40. Alfred K., b. Jan. 3, 1865; m. Oct. 23, 1890, Mary Goddard.
41. Jessie I., b. Jan. 21, 1868.
42. May, b. July 21, 1870.

VI. ROBERT, JR., (31), was born Dec. 6, 1841; married,   , Sadie Ten Eyck.

Children.

43. Sadie, b.   ; m.

VI. ABRAHAM C., (32), was born Sept. 8, 1844; married Oct. 23, 1867, Lizzie F. Lovejoy. He is president of the Prince Manufacturing Co., No. 71 Maiden Lane,

New York, N. Y. (See his brother David, (28). Their father, Robert Prince, was the original manufacturer. Established 1858.

Children.

44. Frederick L., b. Sept. 20, 1868; d. Sept. 24, 1869.
45. Alice, b. Jan. 26, 1874.
46. Persis L., b. Oct. 2, 1876; d. Mar. 10, 1886.
47. Antoinette M., b. May 5, 1881.
48. Melinda C., b. Oct 29, 1883.
49. Florence Louise, b. Nov. 23, 1885.

VI. ANTOINETTE, (33), was born Sept. 19, 1846; m. , Alexander Bass.

Children.

50. William L., b.

RICHARD JOHNSTON PRINCE, AND HIS DESCENDANTS.

I. RICHARD JOHNSTON PRINCE was born in England, Sept. 14, 1797; died Mar. 5, 1840. aged 43 years; married   , Elizabeth ———, who was born in England, Dec. 22, 1796; died Aug. 18, 1832, aged 36 years.

Children.

2. Richard, b. in England, Aug. 19, 1819; d. in Philadelphia, Penn., July 15, 1868, aged 49 years.
3. Sarah, b. in England, June 4, 1822; d. in Philadelphia, Sept. 24, 1884.
4. Anthony, b. in England, Sept. 13, 1824; d. there,———.
5. John, b. in England, Dec. 20, 1826; d. there, Jan. 9, 1828.
6. Thomas, b. in England, Nov. 20, 1828; d. in Philadelphia, Aug. 8, 1893.
7. Rebecca, b. in England, Dec. 31, 1830; d. in Philadelphia, Mar. 26, 1892.

II. RICHARD, (2), was born Aug. 19, 1819, in Carlisle, Cumberland Co., England; died in Philadelphia, Penn., July 15, 1868, aged 49 years; married Mar. 23, 1846, by the Rev. George A. Durburrow, Ann Wilson, who was born Aug. 4, 1825, in Carlisle, Cumberland Co., England, and died Mar. 18, 1884, in Philadelphia, aged 59 years.

Children.

8. Joseph, b. July 19, 1847; d. Aug. 24, 1861, in Philadelphia.
9. Elizabeth, b. June 10, 1849; d. Dec. 25, 1871, in Philadelphia.
10. Margaret, b. June 21, 1851.
11. George, b. Oct. 23, 1853.
12. Richard Johnston, b. Dec. 29, 1855.
13. Robert, b. June 12, 1858.
14. William, b. Mar. 18, 1861.
15. Joseph Wilson, b. Aug. 29, 1863; d. May 9, 1864, in Philadelphia.
16. Samuel Lincoln, b. June 18, 1865.

Above children all born in Philadelphia.

II. ANTHONY, (4), was born in England, Sept. 13, 1824. He left home when about sixteen years of age, and his parents heard nothing from him for years. The last letter received from him was dated Jan. 5, 1879, and his address at that time was New Axminster, Devon, near the School Beer, England. He married previous to 1866, in England, Louisa ———, who was born   , and died there,   . Had five children of which we have the record of only four.

Children.

17. Herbert Atcliffe, b.   , 1866, in England.
18. Ernest, b.   , in England.
19. Annie Sarah, b. Jan. 25, 1877.
20. Louisa, b.   , 1878.

III. GEORGE, (11), was born Oct. 23, 1853, in Philadelphia, Penn.; married there, Nov. 24, 1874, at the parsonage of the Hancock St. M. E. Church, by the Rev. G. G. Rakestraw, Susie Cole, who was born Feb. 28, 1852, in Philadelphia.

Children.

21. George Ellwood, b. Dec. 20, 1876.
22. Ethel Grace, b. Nov. 27, 1881.
23. Adaline Elizabeth, b. July 2, 1891.

Children born in Philadelphia.

III. RICHARD JOHNSTON, (12), was born Dec. 29, 1855, in Philadelphia, Penn.; married first, Mar. 8, 1883, at the M. E. Church parsonage, at Stroudsbury, Penn., by the Rev. George Heacock, Maggie Gordon, who was born Mar. 21, 1860, at Stroud township, Monroe Co., Penn. She died at Philadelphia, June 8, 1888, aged 28 years. He married second, May 15, 1894, Cora Cassidy, who was born,———.

Children by First Wife.

24. Susanna, b. Dec. 30, 1883, in Stroudsbury, Penn.
25. Mabel, b. June 21, 1886, in Philadelphia.

Children by Second Wife.

26. Emma May, b. Feb. 7, 1896, in Philadelphia.

III. ROBERT, (13), was born June 12, 1858, in Philadelphia, Penn.; married there, June 15, 1887, at 2424 East Norris St., by Rev. Henry Beale, pastor of the First Presbyterian Church, Maggie E. Young, who was born June 15, 1866, in Philadelphia.

Children.

27. Florence May, b. Aug. 16, 1888, in Philadelphia.

III. WILLIAM, (14), was born Mar. 18, 1861, in Philadelphia, Penn.; married there,   , at 2311 Jasper St., by Rev. S. A. Blum, pastor Fifth Moravian Church, Martha Stringer, who was born Sept. 18, 1862, in Huddersfield, England.

Children.

28 Ada, b. Aug. 4, 1886, in Philadelphia, Penn.
29. William Harrison, b. Dec. 27, 1888, in Philadelphia.

III. SAMUEL LINCOLN, (16), was born June 18, 1865, in Philadelphia, Penn.; married there June 19, 1889, at No. 1916 East York St., by Rev. James H. Marr, pastor of Beacon Presbyterian Church, Mary Shaw, who was born Aug. 25, 1866, in Philadelphia.

Children.

30. Joseph Craig, b. July 27, 1890.
31. Samuel Richard, b. Oct. 24, 1892.
32. Matthew Shaw, b. Dec. 8, 1894.

Above children born in Philadelphia.

For the benefit of those who shall follow after me I hereby append the following records:—[Author].

In the "Charlestown, (Mass), Genealogies," by Wyman, on page 778, is mentioned a Richard Prince as having been admitted as an inhabitant, with T. Larkin as security, Feb. 1, 1674; also one or two other Princes. In "Griffin's Journal", published at Orient, Long Island, N. Y., in 1857, by Augustus Griffin, is the following: "James and John Prince were brothers. John settled in Southold, where he died in 1675 aged 78 years. Do not know whether James ever came to America. Joseph was John's son, born 1719; died in 1805. There were other sons,—Joseph, Benjamin and Thomas. John Prince, the first son, had three sons,— John, Ezra, and Morton. Ezra died in 1824; his wife was Phebe Horton, by whom he had two sons,—Albert and Orrin; also daughters,—Martha, Betsey, Lucretia, Phebe and Ann. Orrin, born 1816, married Maria L. Welles, 1839."

There was a Richard Prince admitted a freeman at Salem, Dec. 27, 1642; a Samuel Prince, at Hull, May 8, 1678; and also a Samuel Prince, at Hull, May 9, 1680.

Richard Prince and Sarah Rix, of Salem, were married Dec. 25, 1677, and had children:—

    Richard, b. Jan. 21, 1678.
    Joseph, b. Dec. 28, 1680; d. Sept. 14, 1691.
    John, b. Sept. 15, 1682.

The following notice appeared in THE BOSTON DAILY ADVERTISER, Wednesday morning, September 11, 1844, The ADVERTISER copying from the Philadelphia NORTH AMERICAN, and they from the LONDON TIMES.

Copied *verbatim et literatim*, by the author, F. A. Prince, Danielson, Conn.

JAMES PRINCE, DECEASED, HEIR-AT-LAW WANTED.

Any person who can establish their claim to be heir-at-law of James Prince, formerly of Oxford, afterwards of London, cooper, and who died at Hoxton, in 1774, will hear of something greatly to his or her advantage by addressing a letter to J. Waterlow, 24 Birchin Lane, London.

James Prince's brothers were named Edward, Joseph and John. Edward Prince formerly carried on the business of a cooper in London, and is supposed to have immigrated to America about the year 1736, at which period he had four children, named Mary, James, Edward and Joseph.

Any person giving information which may lead to the discovery of the descendants of the said Edward Prince will be rewarded for their trouble. Persons reading this advertisement and acquainted with any one by the name of Prince are requested to draw their attention to it.

In the History of Gloucester, Mass., by John J. Babson, page 129, is the following:—

Thomas Prince is called brother-in-law of Thomas Skillings. He came to Gloucester before 1650 and settled at the Harbor, on what is now Front St., where the family continued to reside more than a hundred years. He also had land in Fisherman's Field. He had a wife, Margaret, who died Feb. 24, 1706. He died Jan. 17, 1690, aged 71, leaving an estate of £153. His children were Thomas, born 1650; John 1653; Mary 1658; and Isaac, 1663. Thomas

Prince, Jr., married Elizabeth Haraden, Sept. 27, 1676, and died Jan. 11, 1705, leaving children,—Edward, Elizabeth, John, Isaac, Sarah, Abigail. Of these, John became a sea captain, and died April 19, 1767, aged 90 years. He married first, Abigail Ellery; married second, Mary, widow of Elder James Sayward, and had eight children,—John, Isaac, Mary and five other daughters. John died young. Isaac married Honor, daughter of Richard Tarr, and they had Sarah and John. This John married Mary, daughter of Jonathan Haskell, in 1755, and they had Mary, born in Gloucester, Aug. 20, 1758; John, born in New Gloucester, Me., Jan. 20, 1761.

John and Isaac, sons of Thomas Prince, Sr., do not appear to have been married in town. Isaac received a soldier's lot at Kettle Cove, in 1679, instead of John, and was here ten years later, but afterwards disappeared. Isaac, son of Thomas Prince, Jr., born in 1683, is supposed to be the same who married Honor Wonson, widow, in 1730. The only male issue of this marriage recorded is a John, born in 1734; he is perhaps the only settler of New Gloucester, Me., of that name. No descendants of Thomas Prince bearing the name have resided in Gloucester for many years.

The following record of Samuel Prince was found on Town Records in Amherst, Mass., which is all there is in regard to Samuel:

Children of Samuel and Irene Moody Prince.

Sophia, b. Dec. 21, 1787.
Samuel, b. Dec. 4, 1789.
Samuel, b. Nov. 27, 1791.
Irene, b. Apr. 2, 1794.
Eri, b. June 23, 1796.
Fanny, b. May 24, 1798.
Asahel, b. Mar. 29, 1800.
Beulah, b. Mar. 20, 1803.

Children of Samuel and Abigail Prince.

Fanny Williams, b. July 28, 1827.
Harry Baxter, b. Mar. 18, 1833.

For the benefit of the readers, and especially to those who wish to further collect, publish and gather into completeness the records of the Prince family, the following information may be of service:—

Capt. Howard L. Prince, Washington, D. C., has collected quite a considerable of Prince material.

Freeman Bradford Prince, 289 Commercial St., Salem, Oregon, has a large amount of information on line of Thomas Prince, of Gloucester, Cape Ann, Massachusetts Bay, Essex Co.

Frederick W. Prince, Hartford, Conn., (with Gatling Gun Co.,) has quite an amount on line of "Elder John," of Hull, of whom he is a descendant.

John T. Prince, Joy St., Boston, Mass., has in Mss. quite a full and complete record of Capt. Job and wife, Elizabeth.

Capt. Greenleaf Cilley, U. S. N., and his brother, Gen. Jona P. Cilley, Rockland, Me., have Prince records.

Thomas Prince, Esq., Boston, Mass., former publisher of The Mass. Historical Genealogical Register, has Prince records in Mss.

Col. Edward Prince, Quincy, Ill., has in Mss., and is still collecting for a genealogy. Hope the near future may bring its presence to the present generation for perusal which are so deeply interested in the records of their ancestors.

RECORDS OF OTHER PRINCE FAMILIES.

The author of this volume, F. A. Prince, Danielson, Conn., has in his possession quite a collection of Prince records, not herein contained, of value to any one who is contemplating a complete genealogy of the Prince family.

George Prince, of the sixth generation, published a pamphlet of 32 pages, in Feb., 1888, on line of "Elder John" Prince, of Hull, Mass., which is a very valuable help to the genealogist. Printed by C. W. Symonds, Boston, Mass.

A well-bound book of 27 pages, containing a memorial of the Rev. Ammi Cushing Prince, being a report of the funeral services and also his obituary, by Rev. George D. Lindsay, was printed in 1895 by Hunt & Eaton, 150 Fifth Avenue, New York.

The New England Magazine for Feb., 1894, published by Warren F. Kellogg, 5 Park Sqr., Boston, Mass., contains "Twelve Hundred Miles on Horseback One Hundred Years Ago," from the Diary of Hezekiah Prince, by George Prince, being an account of Hezekiah Prince's adventures on horseback one hundred years ago. The magazine contains 12 pages of this very valuable old record.

A souvenir is in possession of the author containing a complete account of the gathering of many descendants of Hezekiah and Isabella Prince, of Thomaston, Me., at Spencer, Mass., Aug. 20 to 30, 1891.

For other works, containing the name of Prince, consult "Index to American Genealogies," Fourth Edition, 1895, by Joel Munsell's Sons, Pubs., Albany, N. Y.

CORRECTIONS.

On page 50, near bottom of page, Julia Ballard should be Julius Ballard, d. Jan. 9, 1844, aged 17 months and 17 days.

ADDITIONAL RECORDS.

On page 21, number 17, Solomon Prince. Following is inscription on gravestone: "In memory of Mr. Solomon Prince, who died Feb. ye 8th, A. D. 1767, aged 60 years."

ADDITIONAL RECORDS.

REMARKS.

INDEX.

BY THE NAME OF PRINCE.

Aaron, 43, 58, 87, 88, 89.
Abel, Capt., 44.
Abel, 15, 20, 22, 24, 32, 33, 34, 48, 49, 70.
Abiah, 7, 10.
Abigail, 16, 25, 47, 126.
Abigail M., 54, 68, 69.
Abraham C., 117, 118.
Ada, 123.
Adaline Elizabeth, 122.
Adelaide Edwards, 66.
Adelaide, 118.
Adelaide B., 118.
Albert, 51, 69, 73, 74, 98, 103, 124.
Albert Willard, 60.
Alfred B., 118.
Alfred K., 118.
Alice, 106, 119.
Alice Maria, 80, 91.
Almira, 46, 61, 66, 92.
Alpheus, 35, 46, 65.
Alva T., 87.
Alva Thomas, 109.
Amanda M., 107.
Amasa, 43, 61.
Amasa Tourtellotte, 62.
Ammi Rev. Cushing, 128.

Amos, 15, 25, 44, 45, 46.
Amy Grace, 109.
Ann, 124.
Anna, 7, 9, 21, 22, 27.
Anna F., 108, 112.
Anne, 26.
Annie Maria, 53, 82.
Annie, 59, 62.
Annie Sarah, 121.
Ann Caroline, 54.
Ann Maria, 69.
Anthony, 120, 121.
Antoinette, 117, 119.
Antoinette M., 119.
Arthur Leslie, 110.
Asa Capt., 17, 27.
Asa, 38, 39, 41, 52, 78, 79, 80.
Asahel, 126.

Basil, 105.
Benjamin, 117, 124.
Benjamin Moulton, 95, 110.
Bertha May, 81, 105.
Beulah, 126.
Betty, 24.
Betsey, 6, 25, 44, 45, 62, 64, 124.

(133)

Caleb, 25, 45.
Caleb Strong, 45.
Candis M., 65.
Carrie, 92.
Caroline, 58, 61, 86, 88, 92, 108.
Catherine, 94.
Catherine H., 67.
Catherine J., 108.
Chandler, 46.
Charity, 14.
Charlotte, 45.
Charles, 6.
Charles Edwin, 66.
Charles Henry, 61, 74, 94, 99, 100, 110.
Charles H., 90.
Charles Swan, 109, 113.
Chester, 46.
Clara A., 108, 112.
Clara Jeannette, 95.
Clarence A., 108.
Clifton H., 96.
Cynthia Jane, 54.

Daisy, 92.
Daniel, 5, 6, 16, 26, 43, 52, 56, 58, 79, 104.
Dave, 46.
David, 14, 15, 16, 18, 19, 26, 35, 43, 44, 46, 52, 61, 63, 64, 67, 92, 93, 94, 95, 96, 117, 118.
David L., 96.
David Lucian, 91.
Deidamia, 44, 63.
Dell Sophia, 59, 89.
Dolly, 46.
Dulsenia, 46, 67.

Ebenezer, 19, 31, 32, 33, 34.
Edgar L., 11.
Edward, 64, 69, 117, 125, 126, 127.
Edward, Jr., 64.
Edward Wesley, 94.
Edwin L., 109.
Edith Ellsworth, 64.
Eli, 35.
Ella, 92.
Ella May, 109.
Ella Lovina, 8, 11, 22.
Eliza, 117.
Elizabeth, 6, 7, 8, 12, 13, 15, 19, 20, 23, 27, 28, 31, 36, 65, 115, 116, 120, 121, 126, 127.
Elizabeth Frances, 55, 85.
Elizabeth Preston, 45.
Elmira, 52, 54, 80.
Elmira J., 86, 107.
Elliott, 60, 91, 109, 110.
Elsie, 47, 68.
Elzaphan, 45, 65.
Emily, 6, 69, 70, 96.
Emily M., 79, 104.
Emeline, 61.
Emenette, 93.
Emma May, 122.
Ephraim, 6.
Ernest, 121.
Ernest E., 11.

Ernest Paul, 110.
Ernest William, 80.
Eri, 126.
Ethel, 112.
Ethel Louise, 79.
Ethel Grace, 122.
Eunice, 23, 32, 33, 34, 35, 45, 70.
Evie, 112.
Eva S., 96.
Eva M., 112.
Ezra, 17, 124.

Fanny, 126.
Fanny Tucker, 59, 89.
Fanny Williams, 127.
Fannie Lucetta, 80.
F. A., 12, 125, 128.
Fidelia Maria, 66.
Florence, 93.
Florence L., 10.
Florence Louise., 119.
Florence May, 122.
Florence Turley, 105.
Francis, 105.
Francis Albert, 74, 98, 110.
Franklin Tracy, 8, 10.
Freeman, 47, 69.
Freeman Bradford, 127.
F. W., 42.
Frederick A., 118.
Frederick L., 119.
Frederick W., 127.

George, 48, 49, 56, 67, 70, 97, 121, 128.
George Elliott, 91, 110.
George Francis, 52.
George F., 97.
George E., 107, 111.
George Dickinson, 109.
George Ellwood, 122.
George Frederick, 65.
George Vernon, 94.
George W., 54.
George William, 55.
George Washington, 117.
Georgianna, 67, 70, 95.
Gladys, 112.
Gracy N., 96.

Hannah, 20, 22, 24, 25, 26, 45.
Hannah Plimpton, 53, 82.
Hannah Barker, 6.
Hannah Stiles, 55.
Harriett, 60, 117.
Harriett, N., 60.
Harriett Searls, 65.
Harry Baxter, 127.
Harry W., 11.
Harry Leon, 80.
Harley, 109.
Harvey, 60, 90.
Hattie Rebecca, 91.
Henry, 65.
Henry S., 67, 96.
Henry James, 7, 8.

Henry Rootes Jackson, 84, 105.
Henry W., 109.
Henry Warren, 66.
Herbert Eugene, 94.
Herbert Atcliffe, 121.
Hezekiah, 128.
Horace, 43, 60, 90.
Howard L. (Capt.), 127.
Huldah, 15, 24, 26, 43, 44, 56, 57.

Irene (Moody), 126.
Irene, 126.
Isaac, 125, 126.
Isadore, 54.
Isabella, 128.

James, 6, 7, 12, 13, 14, 15, 25, 45, 46, 124, 125.
James F., 86, 108, 112.
James Moulton, 95, 110.
James G., 118.
James Monroe, 53.
James M., 65.
Jamie, 107.
Jane, 51.
Jane Maria, 8, 11.
Jemima, 39, 41, 53.
Jennie, 92.
Jerome, 70, 97.
Jerusha Jacobs, 72, 74, 103.
Jessie I., 118.

John, 15, 16, 21, 24, 25, 32, 41, 44, 46, 49, 115, 120, 124, 125, 126.
John Adams, 53, 81, 105.
John W., 52.
John Whitney, 79, 105.
John Dudley, 79, 105.
John M., 85, 86, 107.
John Earl, 105.
John S., 106, 111.
John C., 109.
John "Elder", 127, 128.
John Ellsworth, 64.
John Allen, 65.
John T., 127.
Job "Capt", 127.
Jonathan, 14, 26, 27, 35, 46, 56, 86, 108.
Jonathan, Dr., 16.
Joseph, 7, 12, 13, 14, 15, 17, 18, 19, 20, 22, 23, 25, 27, 28, 30, 31, 44, 45, 47, 63, 94, 121, 124, 125.
Joseph, Jr., 53, 82.
Joseph Craig, 123.
Joseph Nelson, 54.
Joseph Wilson, 121.
Joshua, 41.
Julia, 46, 50.
Juliet, 54.
Julius, 129.

K——

Laura S., 86, 107.
Leslie H., 111.
Lewis S., 67, 95.
Lewis Edgar, 8, 10.
Leona, 107.
Lilla, 97.
Lilla B., 97.
Linus, 61, 93.
Luce, 23
Lucretia, 124.
Lucian, 60, 91.
Lucina, 59.
Luella, 93, 107.
Lucy, 32, 43, 44, 48, 49, 60, 62, 70.
Lucy H., 94.
Lucy Maria, 44.
Lucy M., 86.
Luke Packard, 6.
Louis Elliott, 74.
Louisa, 52, 58, 88, 121.
Loren, 70, 97.
Lovina, 7, 10.
Lydia, 26, 46.
Lyman, 39, 41, 48, 49, 70, 96, 97.
Lyman Wilson, 60.

Mabel, 122.
Mary, 16, 17, 19, 20, 27, 34, 42, 47, 48, 52, 65, 69, 78, 115, 117, 125, 126.
Mary Abbott, 64.
Mary Ann, 56, 63, 70.
Mary E., 86, 108.
Mary Ella, 80.
Mary Elizabeth, 90.
Mary Healy, 53, 81, 82.
Mary Jane, 46.
Mary Louisa, 8, 10.
Mary L., 109.
Mary Luvan, 87.
Mary M., 117.
Mary Maria, 58, 87.
Mary Ophelia, 73, 98.
Mary Packard, 6.
Mary Raymond, 55.
Marie Jacqueline, 84, 105.
Martha, 15, 124.
Martha Basiline Hillhouse, 84.
Martha Maria, 91, 110.
Margaret, 117, 121.
May, 92, 118.
Matthew Hooper, 65.
Matthew Shaw, 123.
Mehitable, 6.
M. F. Prince & Co., 107.
Melinda C., 119.
Melven J., 108.
Mercy, 50, 72.
Michael, 45.
Milly N., 59, 90.
Millard F., 107.
Miriam, 26.
Molly, 26.
Morton, 124.
Moses, 25, 45.

INDEX

Naomi, 26.
Nancy, 6.
Nancy Ledicia, 87.
Nancy Elizabeth, 109.
Nancy Woodbury, 54.
Nathan, 16, 39, 41, 45, 49, 50, 65, 71, 72, 73, 98.
Nathan Dyer, 99.
Nellie, 93, 97.
Nellie M., 97.
Nora Hannah, 82.

Oliver Hillhouse, 42, 55, 83, 84, 105.
Oliver H., 85.
Orland, 43, 90, 91, 92, 93, 94.
Orland William, 60.
Orrin, 85, 107, 124.
Otis, 46, 60, 66.

Paul Bradford, 113.
Persis L., 119.
Phebe, 24, 124.
Phœbe, 25.
Polly, 6, 25, 41, 43, 44, 51, 57, 59, 62, 64, 77, 78.
Prince, Mr. and Mrs. F. A., 99, 100.
Prince, Mrs. H. E., 69.
Prudence Ann, 64.

Q—

Rachel, 27, 43, 47, 60, 61.
Ray C., 96.
Rebecca, 12, 14, 27, 32, 47, 90, 120.
Rebecca Harriett, 91.
Rebekah, 46, 66.
Richard, 12, 20, 120, 124.
Richard Johnston, 120, 121, 122.
Robert, 12, 13, 14, 17, 18, 19, 20, 27, 31, 38, 39, 40, 41, 49, 52, 53, 73, 81, 82, 115, 117, 119, 121, 122.
Robert Henry, 81.
Robert H., 106.
Robert Jr., 117, 118.
Rose E., 93.
Ruby Luvan, 56.
Ruth, 17, 26, 116.
Ruth Fuller, 45.

Sadie, 118.
Sadie Mabel, 94.
Sally, 6, 50, 62, 71.
Sally Maria, 52.
Samuel, 15, 19, 24, 42, 56, 62, 69, 115, 117, 124, 126.
Samuel, Jr., 116, 117.
Samuel Lincoln, 121, 123.
Samuel Porter, 35.
Samuel Richard, 123.
Sanford, 56, 85, 106, 107, 108.
Sanford C., 87, 108.

Sanford N., 109.
Sarah, 6, 12, 14, 16, 17, 19, 20, 26, 35, 42, 69, 116, 117, 120, 126.
Sarah A., 55, 82.
Sarah Ann, 6.
Sarah Alice, 8, 11.
Sarah E., 60.
Sarah Jane, 61, 67, 93, 95.
Sarah Maria, 7, 84.
Sarah Virginia, 55, 84.
Solomon, 15, 17, 19, 21, 130.
Sophia, 56, 86, 87, 88, 89, 106, 107, 108, 126.
Sophia Ellsworth, 63.
Stephen, 16, 25, 26, 46, 47.
Susanna, 15, 20, 122.
Susannah, 20, 36, 115.

Tamson Murdock, 59.
Thomas, 43, 56, 85, 86, 87, 120, 124, 125, 127.
Thomas, Jr., 126.
Thomas, Sr., 126.
Timothy, 14, 15, 23, 24, 42, 44, 63, 94.
Timothy, Sr., 24.
Timothy, Jr., 24.
Timothy Capt , 43.

Ulysses S., 109.
Uriah Cady, 44, 65.

Vernon, 61, 93.

Walter Everett, 110.
Walter G., 107.
Wilber Joseph, 106, 111.
William, 15, 22, 23, 24, 35, 41, 42, 44, 52, 79, 115, 121, 122.
William Augustus, 117.
William Harrison, 123.
William Henry, 97.
William H., 91, 109, 113.
William S., 85, 106, 111, 112.
William Sanford, 108, 112.
William M., 111.
Willie Asa, 80.
Willie Harvey, 91.
Willard, 43, 48, 49, 59, 90.

X—

Y—

Zeviah, 47, 68.

INDEX

OF NAMES OTHER THAN PRINCE.

Adams, Mrs. Ellen D., 71.
" Michael, 18.
" Lieut. John, 54.
" Mary Elizabeth, 117.
Aiken, Henry, 88.
Ailsworth, Bethania, 60.
Alby, Lucretia J., 79.
Allen, Nancy, 65.
" Charles, 56.
Alton, Moses, 26.
Anthony, Arnold, 68.
" Sarah Jane, 68.
" Julia Ann, 68.
" Sophia, 68.
" Charles Francis, 68.
" Henry Augustus, 68.
" George Edwin, 68.
" Sophia Elizabeth, 68.
Arthur, Mary Virginia, 64.
" James, 64.
" Mary (Reed), 64.
Atwood, Rebecca, 29.
" Elijah, 29, 30, 47.

Babson, John J., 125.

Babcock, James H., 79.
Baker, Leonard, 58.
" Henry A., 23, 41.
" Charles, 53.
" Nettie, 78.
Ballard, Hamilton, 50.
" Julia, 50.
" Leonidas, 50.
Barnes, Ada Louise, 80.
" Annie, 89.
" Amanda, 97.
" Rev. Charles Curtis, 73.
" Charles Merrick, 89.
" Davis Mason, 80.
" Edwin Milton, 80.
" Frank Paine, 89.
" Halsey H., 80.
" Herbert Wesley, 80.
" Hattie Frances, 80.
" James Lincoln, 80.
" Lillian, 79, 105.
" Lucian Milton, 80.
" Merrick, 59, 89.
" William, 97.
Barrett, Anson, 70, 96.
" Ellen, 96.

" Mary, 96, 97.
" Smith, 96.
" William Marsh, 97.
Bartlett, Esther J., 61.
Bass, Alexander, 117, 119.
" Albert R., 117.
" William L., 119.
Bates, Butler, 58.
" H. Davis, 73.
" Ira, 73.
" Orson, 58.
Beale, Rev. Henry, 122.
Bell, Francis, 54.
Belle, Jennie, 61, 92.
Berry, Hannah, 54.
Benson, Alphonso, 53.
" Albert, 53.
" Cornelia, 53.
" Jane Davis, 53.
" Mary Ann, 53.
" Robert Prince, 53.
" Sarah Key, 53.
" Thomas, 40, 53.
" Jemima, 40.
" Thomas, Jr., 53.
Bixby, Aaron, 47, 48.
" Augustus, 52.
" Henry, 110.
" Jemima, 20, 38, 49.
" Joseph, 48.
" Lucy, 48.
" Lillian Flora, 95, 110.
" Nancy, 48.
" Nathan, Jr., 38, 47.
" Nathan, Sr., 38.
" Sally, 48.

" Origin, 52.
Bixbee, Mary, 28, 48.
Blum, Rev. S. A., 122.
Blackstone, Sarah, 53.
Bowers, Edward M., 93.
Bowen, Charles, 93.
Bowen, Isaac, 19.
Boice, Elihu, 9.
Bostwick, T., 55.
Brackett, Asa, 57.
" Dea. Prince, 61.
" Betsey, 57.
" Huldah, 57.
" Roxiliany, 57.
" Mary, 57.
" Prince, 57.
Bradford, Edwin Freeman, 104.
" Bertha Pamele, 105.
" Caroline, 104.
" Caroline (Cummings), 104.
" Fannie Louise, 105.
" Henry, 104.
" Madora, 104.
" William, 104.
" Rev. Mr., 92.
Brewer, Mr., 69.
Bright, Warren Henry, 111.
" Mary Ellen (Peary), 111.
" Annie Bell, 99, 110.
Brown, Rev., 98.
" Rev. Henry, 104.
" Billy, 26.

"   David, 48.
"   Emmons, 104.
"   Jeremiah, 66.
"   Lena, 104.
Brunt, Capt. Tunis B. Van, 116.
Brower, Nicholas B., 116.
Buck, Thomas, 10.
Buckingham, Rev. John A., 95.
Burbank, Phebe, 54.
Burgoyne, Gen., 5.
Burgess, Mary, 115.
Burnett, George A., 78.
Burt, Henry L., 97.
Burrill, Mary, 38, 47.
Buxton, Edward E., 96.
"   George, 81.

Cabot, Rev. Marston, 31, 113.
Cady, David, 20.
"   Joseph, 17.
"   Lucy, 24, 44.
"   Uriah, 24, 44.
Cargill, Antoinette, 117.
Carman, Ruth, 115.
Carriel, Joseph, 26.
"   Jonathan, 32.
Carroll, Mary, 50.
"   Nathaniel, 50.
"   Rebecca, 19, 31.
Carr, Sophia, 56, 85.
Carleton, Benjamin, 77.
Carpenter, Mrs Addie (Hill), 93.

"   Rev. Eber, 89.
"   Emily, 52, 79, 104.
"   Leonard, 79.
"   Matilda (Reynolds), 79.
Cassidy, Cora, 122.
Chaffee, Charles, 99.
"   Sarah Elizabeth, 99.
"   Sarah Maria, 74, 98, 110.
Chandler, Abigail, 80.
"   John, 94.
"   Lucy Manning, 94.
"   Mary, 94.
"   William Bradbury, 80.
"   William, 80.
Chapman, Mrs. Anna T., 47.
Child, Orinda, 36.
Cilley, Capt. Greenleaf, 127.
"   Gen. Jona P., 127.
Clark, Col. Caleb, 116.
Coachman, Rev. M., 108.
Coburn, Henry, 56.
Cole, Sarah M., 68.
"   Susie, 121.
Coman, John, 48, 70.
Comins, Frances A., 117, 118.
"   John P., 118.
Converse, Asa, 18.
"   George, 73.
"   George Franklin, 73.
"   Jesse Franklin, 50, 72.
"   Joel T., 72, 73.

"   Joseph T., 73.
"   Mary E., 73.
Cook, Rev. Rozel, 55.
Copeland, Polly, 33, 34.
"   Phineas, 29, 30, 33, 34, 47.
"   Rachel, 28.
Corbin, Alpheus, 48, 49, 70, 71.
"   Betty, 36.
"   Caroline, 71.
"   Daniel, 36.
"   Capt., 37.
"   Clement, 37.
"   Elijah, 19, 36, 37.
"   Emeline, 71.
"   Eunice Ann, 71.
"   Elbridge, 68.
"   George Alpheus, 71.
"   Harriett, 71.
"   John Prince, 71.
"   Lucy Nichols, 71.
"   Lewis B., 54.
"   Parley, 36.
"   Polly, 70.
"   Schuyler, 36.
Cowen, Fanny, 20.
Crosby, Elijah, 33.
"   Nathaniel, 18, 19, 31.
"   Stephen, 21.
Cross, Anna, 45.

Dailey, Sarah Ellis, 7.
Daniels, George F., 93.
Davis, Clarissa, 57.
"   Harvey, 51, 77.
"   Joshua, 38.

"   Sarah E., 108.
Dawson, Mary Jane, 64, 94.
Day, Alice May, 69.
"   Charles S., 69.
Dennison, Eleaser, 64.
"   John M., 44, 64.
"   Prudence, 44.
"   Thomas, 44.
"   William, 44, 64, 65.
Dempsey, Fred, 93.
Desrosiers, Jennie, 80.
Dillaber, George, 71.
Dodge, R. B., 58.
"   David, 37, 38.
"   Dorcas, 38.
"   Daniel, 36, 37.
"   Paul, 37.
"   Lorain, 38.
"   Mark, 20, 36, 37.
"   Molly, 38.
"   Rufus, 38.
"   Susannah, 37, 38.
"   Thede, 38.
Dow, Rev. Daniel, 50, 52, 53, 57, 59, 70, 71, 77, 113.
Dowes, Hattie S., 11.
Dresser, Jacob, 18.
Dudley, Paul, 37.
Duncklee, Thaddeus, 20.
Durkee, Erastus B., 78.
Durham, Ada, 83.
Durburrow, Rev. Geo. A., 120.
Dwinnell, Henry, 45.
Dyke, Miss S. J., 69.

INDEX.

Eames, Geo. M., 67.
" George P., 68.
" Mary Ann, 67.
Earle, Ellis P., 118.
Eaton, Hannah, 15, 22.
Edwards, Abigail, 58.
" Amy A., 92.
" David G., 92.
" Emily A., 92.
" Horace, 61, 92.
" Horace P., 92.
" Porter, 71.
Edmunds, ——, 89.
Ellenwood, Ralph, 20.
Elliott, Dyer Nichols, 73.
" Eliza (Green), 73.
" Emergene, 72.
" Horace, 71, 78.
" Mary, 43, 56, 71.
" Ophelia, 51, 73, 74, 98, 103.
" Oscaforia J., 72.
" Polly (Dexter), 72.
" Sally, 78.
" Sylvester, 77.
" Theodore, 50, 71.
" Thomas, Jr., 71, 78.
Ellyot, Joseph, 31.
" Joseph, Jr., 32.
Ellery, Abigail, 126.
Ellsworth, Daniel, 63.
" Mary (Abbot), 63.
" Sophia, 44, 63.
Elwell, Charles Barnes, 78.

Elwell, Callie Maria, 78.
" Elizabeth, 78.
" Emily Frances, 78.
" George Francis, 78.
" Jane Louisa, 78.
" Mark, 78.
" Sally Barnes, 78.
" William Clifford, 78.
Emerson, Rev. Warren, 81.
Eyck, Sadie Ten, 117, 118.

Faulkner, Sophia, 43, 58.
Felton, Anne, 26.
" Dorcas, 26.
" Nathaniel, 26.
Fellows, Rev. S. H., 82.
Filmer, Rev. T. T., 103.
Fillmore, Capt. Earl, 116.
Fisk, Melissa A., 97.
Fisher, William. Jr., 38.
Fitch, Mary, 42.
Fitts, Rev. H., 72.
Foster, Arnold, 62.
" John, 32.
" Rev. Festus, 87.
Fox, Capt. Elisha, 42.
Frost, Adaline S., 93.
" Charles E., 93.
" Carrie E., 93.
" George M., 93.
" George W., 93.
" Sarah Gertrude, 93.
Fuller Eunice, 45.
" Phebe, 16.

INDEX. 145

Ganfield, Robert, 14.
Gale, Carrie C., 38.
Gates, Gen., 5.
Gedney, John, 12.
Gibson, Allura, 95.
Gilmore, Caroline Luvan, 88.
" Edwin Oscar, 88.
" Georgiana, 88.
" Henry Sullivan, 88.
" Julia Frances, 88.
" Mary Ann, 88.
" Silas, 58, 88.
" Silas Prince, 88.
Gillet, Addis, 8.
Goddard, Mary, 118.
Goodale, Emma, 17.
" Ebenezer, 25.
" John, 22.
" Joshua, 24.
" Mary, 24.
" Rachel, 24.
Gordon, Maggie, 122.
Gore, Rebecca, 43, 60.
Greene, Dr. James Mercer, 55, 84.
" James Edward Beauregard, 85.
" Jane (McConkey), 84.
" Francis Mitchell, 85.
" Henry McConkey, 84.
" Mary Raymond, 84.
" Oliver Hillhouse, 84.
" Virginia Selina, 85, 106.

Greene, William Montgomery, 84, 85.
Green, Caroline E., 109, 113.
" Charles, 108.
Griffin, Augustus, 124.
Griswold, Sarah, 42.
" John, 42.
Grosvenor, Charles J., 41.
" Lemuel, 31, 34.
" Thomas, 30, 34, 49.
Guild, Mary Stiles (Paul), 54.

Hale, Laura A., 68.
Hall, Ann Judson, 67.
" Ann Jennett, 67.
" Austin, 66.
" Calvin, 66.
" David, 66.
" George Calvin, 66.
" George, 66.
" Jane Judson, 66.
" Judson W., 67.
" Julia E., 67.
" Luvan Maria, 66.
" Nathan Sumner, 66.
Hamm, Isabel, 78.
Hamilton, W. H., 111.
Hansom, Cornelia, 84.
Haraden, Elizabeth, 126.
Harback, Henry, 26.
Harris, Elmer R., 112.
" Fred G., 112.
" Isaac M., 112.

"   Jay B., 112.
"   Nora A., 112.
Hartshorn, Sarah A., 88.
"   John, 20.
Harwood, Catherine, 79.
Haskell, John, 126.
"   Mary, 126.
"   Joseph, 18.
Hatch, B. F., 67.
Haven, Rev., 79.
Hayward, Polly, 25.
"   L. S., 31, 34.
Heacock, Rev. George, 122.
Healy, Hammond, 40.
Heesy, Rev. Phineas, 80.
Helme, Samuel M., 64.
Henry, E., 53.
"   Erastus, 81.
"   Elizabeth (Putnam), 81.
Hewlett, John, 33.
Hiers, Betsey, 65.
Hines, Lewis, 54.
Hinks, Rev. E. F., 81.
Hill, Rev. Dr., 81.
"   Emma, 96.
"   Jane, 106, 111, 112.
"   Jennie E., 111.
Hillhouse, Rev. James, 42.
"   Sarah (Griswold), 42.
"   Judge William, 42.
"   Mary, 42.
Holmes, Abner, 56.
Holton, Judge, 16.
Holland, Elizabeth, 22, 23.

"   Joseph, 22, 23.
"   Mary, 22, 23, 41.
Holt, Sarah (Grace), 55.
Hornbeck, Mary Adelia, 108, 112.
Horton, Phebe, 124.
Howe, Frank Mason, 110.
"   Joseph Gilbert, 110.
Humes, John A., 62.
Humphrey, James, 53.
Hunt, Elizabeth, 7.
Hunt and Eaton, 128.

I—

Jacobs, Abigail, 51, 77.
"   Ann Maria, 77.
"   Addie J., 78.
"   Delia, 51, 77.
"   David, 51.
"   Dinah, 51.
"   Emma Augusta, 78.
"   Esq. John, 51.
"   Ezra, 77.
"   Hannah, 51, 52.
"   Henry Dexter, 78.
"   John, 41, 50, 51, 77, 78.
"   John Elliott, 78.
"   Jerusha, 50, 51.
"   Lorain, 51.
"   Mary, 51, 77.
"   Mary Elizabeth, 78.
"   Marquis, 77.
"   Robert, 52, 78.

INDEX.

Jackson, Sarah, 55.
" Sarah Maria, 83, 84.
" Henry, LL.D., 55.
" Henry, 83.
" Martha, 83.
Jeffrey, James, 17.
Jewett, Rev. David, 22.
" Patience, 22.
Johnson, A. J., 83.
" Augustus, 96.
" Samuel, (Col.), 54.

King, Barrington, 85.
" Barrington James, 85.
" Charles, 85.
" James Roswell, 55, 85.
" Harriet Buell, 85.
" Mary Nephew, 85.
" Oliver Hillhouse, 85.
" Rev. George I, 64.
Kellogg, Warren F., 128.
Kinne, Elizabeth J., 107.

Lamb, Charlotte, 47, 69.
Larkin, T., 124.
Larned, James Edward, 80.
Lee, Hannah, 42.
" Mrs. H. E., 69.
" Harry, 69.
Lindsay, Rev. George D., 128.
Littlefield, Lucy Ann, 61.
Lombard, Lucy O., 97.

Lovell, Edward, 91.
Lovejoy, Lizzie F., 117, 118.
" Nathaniel, 54.
Lowe, Mary E., 80.
Lycett, John J., 11.

Marcy, Charles, 59.
" Fidelia, 81.
" Gurdon, 81.
" Nancy Maria, 53, 81.
" Mary, 59.
" Washington, 59.
McCambridge, Mrs., 89.
McIntyre, Harriett, 91.
McDonald, Maria L., 97.
McConkey, Jane, 84.
Mansfield, Daniel, 37.
Marr, Rev. James H., 123.
May, Dexter, 98.
Maynard, M. A., 68.
Melvin, David, 20.
Merrifield, L. W., 67.
Merritt, Mrs. Mary, 67, 95.
Miller, Amanda, 9.
" Celia Maria, 9.
" Eliza Ann, 9.
" Harriett, 8.
" Josiah, 8, 9.
" John, 9.
" Nancy, 56, 86.
" Sarah, 9.
" William Henry, 9.
Mills, Mindwell, 21.
Mitteer, Ella J., 111.

Moffit, Eleazer, 33, 34.
Montross, Mr., 115.
Moore, Aquilla, 9.
" Mrs. A., 9.
" Miss, 117.
" Allen Francis, 104.
Morse, David, 26.
Moulton, Mary, 65.
Munsell, Joel's Sons, 128.
Murry, Charles Bernard, 69.
" Peleg Freeman, 69.
Mussey, Mary, 21.
" Dr. John, 21.

Newton, Alfred J., 88.
" Charles O., 87.
" Emily M., 88.
" George L., 88.
" John, 58, 87.
" Josiah Hayes, 59.
" Sarah M., 87.
Nichols, Elizabeth, 17, 27.
" John, 15.
" Jonathan, 40, 48, 50.
" Lucy, 32, 48.
" Thomas, 15.
Norman, Mary (Ross), 42, 55.
" George, 55.
Norwood, Mary, 116.

Oliver, Harriett A., 67.
" James, 67.
Ormsbee, Mary 19, 35.
" Solomon, 19, 21, 34, 35.

Osborne, Alexander, 12.
" Sarah, 12.
Osterhout, Rev. J. V., 72.

Pack, Rev. Jabez, 98.
Packard, James, 5.
" Mary, 5, 6.
Palmer, Asenath, 30.
" Flora, 112.
" Herbert S., 112.
Parker, Phebe, 45.
Parsons, Orris, 68.
Partridge, Dea., 7.
" Herbert Graves, 72.
" Rev. Lyman, 72.
" Theodore Elliott, 72.
Pelton, Lovina, 8.
" Merinda, 8.
" Tracy, 8.
Penniman, Rev. G. W., 79.
Perrin, (Lieut.) Daniel, 52.
" Dolly, 36.
" Mary (Dresser), 52.
" Polly, 52.
Perkins, Abigail, 25, 46.
Pester, William, 13.
Phelps, Horatio, 40.
" Lerant, 11.
Phipps, Calvin, 43, 61.
" George Washington, 61.
" Hannah, 41, 52, 81, 82.
" Jason, 30, 52.
" Mary, 61.
" Sarah, 30.

Phillips, David, 115.
" Jacob, 14.
" Silence, 14.
Pierce, Addison, 59, 90.
" Carrie E., 90.
" Caroline, 90.
" Clark M., 90.
" Deidamia, 44.
" Myron L., 90.
" Nathan, 15.
Poe, Edgar Allen, 106.
" Harvey Hillhouse, 106.
" Sarah Virginia, 106.
" Selina (Shirley), 106.
" Shirley, 106.
" Hon. Washington, 106.
" William Ashe, 85, 106.
" Willie, 106.
Popkins, Sarah, 6.
Porter, Eunice, 19, 35.
" Hannah, 35.
" Joseph, 16.
" Mary, 16.
" Samuel, 10, 35.
Potter, Anna, 62.
" Asa, 62.
" Charles J., 92.
" Frank E., 92.
" James F., 92.
" Nichols, 62.
Preston, Elizabeth, 25.
" John, 25.
" Moses, 25.
Putney, Eleazer, 26.
Putnam, Dr. Amos, 14.
" E., 12.

" Hannah, 15, 24, 25.
" Kate Henrietta, 110.
" Capt. John, 12.
" John, 12, 15.
" James, 24.
" Joshua, 24.
" Russell, 110.
" Thomas, 12.

Q—

Rakestraw, Rev. G.G., 121.
Rand, Amanda, 67, 96.
Raymond, Joshua, 23.
" Mary, 23.
Rea, Elizabeth, 16, 26.
" Sarah, 14.
Reddin, Thomas, 14.
Reddington, David, 21.
Rice, Carrie, 10.
" Carrie J., 10.
" Charles L., 10.
" Eugene H., 10.
" Frank T., 10.
" Frederick W., 10.
" Henry, 10.
" Louisa, 9.
" Willard A., 10.
Richardson, Arthur Francois, 103.
" Bertha Carroll, 104.
" Edward Francois, 74, 103.
" Charles B., 68.
" John S., 53.

Richardson, Lillian Rosamond, 104.
" Louis Earnest, 104.
" Rev. M., 93, 110.
Richard, Wm., 19.
Richmond, Allen Barber, 73, 98.
Rix, Sarah, 124.
Roby, Benjamin, 20.
Robbins, Emily F., 94.
" Daniel, 64.
Robinson, Katy D., 69.
" Elizabeth, 14, 17, 22.
Rogers, Abigail, 16.
" Adeline, 60.
" Adeline, 94.
" Hannah, 90.
" Jane M., 9, 11.
" Julia Ann, 9.
" Levi H., 9.
" Orrin, 9.
" Sarah M., 61, 93.
Rollins, Elizabeth, 20.
Ross, Martha Jane, 108.
Russell, Rev. Noadiah, 27, 32, 35, 36, 43, 47, 48, 49, 113.
Ruwee, John, 17.
" Job, 17.

Sanger, Rev. J. G., 104.
Sanderson, Rev. Alonzo, 11, 105.
Sargent, Dr. C. S., 78.
Sayward, Elder James, 126.
" Mary, 126.

Schmohl, J. G., 81, 105.
Scarborough, Henrietta, 44, 63.
" Herbert, 63.
" Francis A., 63.
" Lucy Prince, 63.
" Mary (Amidon), 63.
" Phillip, 44, 63.
" Samuel, 44, 63.
" Theodore, 63.
Searles, Alexander, 69.
Secomb, Daniel F., 21.
Sellard, Julia, 83.
Sharrock, Mattie, 112.
Shaw, Mary, 123.
Sherman, George, 87.
" John, 87.
" John A., 87.
" Lewis, 87.
" Roger, 87.
Shumway, Betsey, 73.
" John, 73.
" David, 26.
" Ebenezer, 26, 46.
" Rebekah, 26, 46.
Sibley, Daniel, 25.
Sinclair, Horace B., 93.
Skillings, Margaret, 125.
" Thomas, 125.
Sleeper, Rev., 96.
Smiley, Rev. Edward, 110.
Smith, Ada May, 11.
" Mrs. C. H., 8.
" Charles Henry, 11.
" Alexander Nichols, 82.

INDEX. 151

Souls, Sarah Elizabeth, 53.
Starr, Comfort, 27.
" Elizabeth, 19, 27.
Stebbins, Laura L., 10.
Sterns, Austin, 88.
" Lizzie Frances, 88.
Stephenson, Sarah R., 10.
" Wm. G., 10.
Stewart, George Freemont, 56.
" John, 56.
Stiles, Cyrus, 54.
" Hannah Curtis, 54.
Stringer, Martha, 122.
Sturdevant, Rose E., 112.
Stone, Annie, 43, 59.
" Caroline M., 89.
" Eliza M., 89.
" George Sullivan, 89.
" John, 18.
" Lucella W., 95.
" Sullivan, 58, 88.
" P. Bason, 19.
" Samuel, 21.
Sucese, Jasmine, 83.
" Jay B., 83.
" Jennie, 83.
" John M., 55, 82.
" John Prince, 83.
" Joseph Hahnemann, 83.
" Josie M., 83.
" Sarah A. (Prince), 54.
Symonds, C. W., 128.
" Phebe, 17, 27, 31, 34.
Sylvester, Levi, 18.

Sweetser, Rev. Sanford B., 110.

Taber, Rhoda, 59.
Tague, John R., 83.
Tarr, Richard, 126.
" Honor, 126.
Thayer, Clifford M., 11.
" Dwight, 9.
" Mrs. Lewis, 9.
" Lewis, 11.
" Leon Dowes, 11.
" Levi L., 11.
Thatcher, Anna M., 109, 113.
" Rev. S., 113.
Thompson, Asenath, 58.
" Augusta, 58.
" Betsey (Studley), 82.
" Elijah, 43, 57.
" E. F., 53.
" Edward Freeman, 82.
" Hiram, 82.
" John Dresser, 57.
" John, 57.
" Letey, 58.
" Polly, 58.
" Thomas Elliott, 57.
" Tyler, 58.
Thomas, Rev. James S., 73.
" Jordan Sumner, 84, 105.
" Florence, 106.
" Mary (Sumner), 105.
" Mary Sumner, 106.
" Marie Jacqueline, 106.

INDEX.

" Sarah Prince, 106.
" William George, 105, 106.
Thorne, Ann, 115.
Titus, Sarah J., 95, 110.
Tourtellotte, Barnabus, 58.
    " Mahala, 43, 62.
    " Thankful, 43, 58.
Town, Archelaus, 49.
    " Dyer, 33, 49.
    " Ebenezer, 33, 49.
    " Isaac, 49.
    " John, 33, 49.
    " Lucy, 49.
    " Rebecca, 33, 49.
    " Roby, 49.
    " Sarah, 49.
    " Solomon, 14.
    " William, 40, 49.
Townsend, Charlotte, 81.
Trask, Capt. William, 13.
Tupper, Henry, 54.
Turley, John, 84, 105.
    " Marie Jane, 84, 105.
    " Mary, 84, 105.
Twiss, Abbie, 69.
    " Amos, 69.
    " James F., 47, 68.
    " Jennison, 26.
    " Stephen, 68.

Upham, Hon. C. W., 13.
    " Mrs. C. E., 13.

Vanderbilt, Mrs. Emeline M., 86.
    " Ellen, 86.
    " Louisa, 86.
Vinton, Emeline, 90.
    " Patty, 26, 46.

Wadsworth, Lois, 66.
Wakefield, Tamer, 38.
Wallace, Etta, 78.
Walker, Bessie A., 96.
    " Charles F., 95.
    " David H., 96.
    " Hattie L., 95.
    " Florence A., 96.
    " Ida J., 96.
    " William, 67, 95.
    " William A., 67.
    " Warren A., 95.
Walworth, Reuben H., 42.
Ward, Dea., 98.
Wardwell, William, 62.
Warren, Sarah, 12.
Warren's General, 108.
Waterlow, J., 125.
Webster, John, 37.
Weld, Mary F., 88.
Welles, Maria L., 124.
West, Marcus, 8.
White, Levi, 18.
    " Rhoda, 37.
Whittemore, Lyman, 36.
    " Sarah, 36.
    " William, 19, 35, 36.
Wiat, George, 24.

Williams, Charles G., 22.
" Capt. Jerome W., 23.
" Emma, 91.
" Mary, 22.
" William, 23.
Wilson, Ann, 120.
Winter, Gabriel, 116.
Wonson, Honor, 126.
Woodbury, Rev. A., 109.
Worthington, Rev. W. A., 77.
Wright, James, 7.
" Joseph, 7, 54.

" Justus, 7.
Wyatt, Sarah, 20, 53.

X—

Young, Aaron Prince, 89.
" Frank Ripley, 89.
" James R., 59, 89.
" John W., 78.
" Linus Childs, 89.
" Maggie., E., 122.

Z—

www.ingramcontent.com/pod-product-compliance
Lightning Source LLC
Chambersburg PA
CBHW020244170426
43202CB00008B/226